A Memoir in Short Stories

One Summer in My Life

Manijeh Badiozamani

HALLARD
PRESS

ONE SUMMER IN MY LIFE: A Memoir in Short Stories
Copyright © 2021 Manijeh Badiozamani   All rights reserved.

Cover Design, Typography & Production by Hallard Press LLC/John W Prince

Published by Hallard Press LLC.
www.HallardPress.com   Info@HallardPress.com   352-234-6099
Bulk copies of this book can be ordered at Info@HallardPress.com

Publisher's Cataloging-in-Publication data

Names: Badiozamani, Manijeh, author.
Title: One summer in my life / Manijeh Badiozamani.
Description: The Villages, FL: Hallard Press, LLC, 2021.
Identifiers: LCCN: 2021911707 | ISBN: 978-17328561-4-1 (paperback) | 978-1-7328561-5-8 (ebook)
Subjects: LCSH Badiozamani, Manijeh. | Women--Iran--Biography. | Iranian American women--Biography. | Iranian Americans--Biography. | United States--Social life and customs. | BISAC BIOGRAPHY & AUTOBIOGRAPHY / Personal Memoirs | BIOGRAPHY & AUTOBIOGRAPHY / Cultural, Ethnic & Regional / Arab & Middle Eastern | BIOGRAPHY & AUTOBIOGRAPHY / Women
Classification: LCC E184.I5 .B32 2021 | DDC 973/.0491550092--dc23

Printed in the United States of America   1

ISBN: 978-1-7328561-4-1 (Paperback)
ISBN: 978-1-7328561-5-8 (Ebook)

DEDICATION

To the memory of Dottie and Ray Fisher

Table of Contents

Preface

Know then thyself, presume not God to scan,

The proper study of mankind is man.

Alexander Pope

Frankly, I don't know if it was Rabbi Reb Zebulun, or Isaac Bashevis Singer who first said: "Today we live, but by tomorrow, today will be a story. The whole world, all human life, is one long story."

It is so true; life stories are all around us. I find my own life to be a story with many chapters. People appear and disappear; events happen. I make decisions, endure hardship, set goals for myself, have dreams and aspirations. I experience disappointments as well as moments of exaltation. Humorous encounters, surprises, reprimands, and compliments—these are all part of my life journey. And when I turn around and look back at the road behind, I marvel.

Wow, did I come all this way?

When I was an undergraduate at the University of Tehran, I took a class on how to read poetry. We used a textbook written by Roy Thomas, published by University of London Press. My professor, Olive Suratgar, taught me how to appreciate poetry and how to read a poem and analyze it. Not that I was unfamiliar with poetry—Hafez, Saadi, Ferdowsi, and Rumi are some of the great Persian poets, and I had read their work off and on as assignments in school. But reading English poetry and enjoying it, was something I had to learn and cultivate.

I recall in that class we began with Shakespeare's sonnets and moved on to Wordsworth, Shelley, and Keats. I don't remember everything that we discussed in that class, but certain lines of certain poems still stick in my mind today, like these from a poem by William Wordsworth:

> "Though nothing can bring back the hour
> Of splendor in the grass, of glory in the flower;
> We will grieve not, rather find
> Strength in what remains behind;"

The 1961 movie, *Splendor in the Grass*, in which Natalie Wood and Warren Beatty portray teenage love, might have also contributed to my lasting memory of those lines. I saw the movie in Tehran.

We then moved on to T.S. Elliot, and "The Love Song of J. Alfred Prufrock." For some odd reason, the line in which he laments, "I grow old . . . I grow old . . . I shall wear the bottoms of my trousers rolled" has forever stuck in my brain—and I was twenty-one years old when I first read it!

I labored over interpreting *The Waste Land* and tried to figure out the metaphors, references, and allusions. I learned enough about the rhythm, rhyme, poetic style, and figurative language to get a passing grade in that course.

But it was Alexander Pope's *An Essay on Man*, that made a lasting impression on me—human beings are a bundle of duality and confusion. Socrates said, "To know thyself is the beginning of wisdom," and Rumi said something like, "You are searching the world for treasure, but the real treasure is yourself."

My life's journey of living in two continents, has not only given me exciting challenges, it has also made me to accept the manifestation of God's larger plans in my life. What the future holds is unknown to all, but what is known to me are the stories thus far. Writing them down is my way of knowing who I am. As humans, we are a paradox of sorts: we can reason, and we can be ignorant at times; we will have highs and lows. But one truth I've learned about myself is my unwavering interest in, and love for, human beings and their life stories.

Enjoy these stories, then write your own. Rest assured, they will be fascinating.

Introduction

A Different Sort of Life

In July of 1979 I wrote the following "autobiography" to submit along with my application to a law school in Indianapolis. It was over forty-two years ago. Everything I put down in this autobiography is precisely what I had done up to that point in my life. I chuckle when I read it today. Did I sound arrogant and self-promoting? Could I have worded it differently? Could I have used a softer tone? It's a sign of maturity when we can look back and chuckle!

I wonder what the admission counselors at the law school thought of me when they read it! Today, it sounds more like a resume to me. I was not accepted to that law school, and shortly thereafter, we moved from Indiana to Idaho.

I'm the eldest of three girls and grew up in a comfortable middle-class family in Tehran, Iran. My parents placed great importance on education and have instilled in me a sense of responsibility to work to my fullest potential. As a result, throughout my educational experience I have ranked at the highest level of my classes.

In 1961, I was awarded an American Field Service Scholarship, giving me the opportunity to study as a high school senior at Avon Lake High School in Ohio for one year. This experience helped me learn about American family life, American society, and its social and political system. *(Stories and experiences from this particular year will be the subject of another book:* A Year in Middle America.*)*

In 1963, I entered the University of Tehran, College of Letters and Humanities, where I was able to sit and pass the first year's examinations, admitting me to the second-year program immediately. In June of 1965, I graduated with honors and ranked first in my graduating class. In the final year, I was elected president of the Girls' Association, a newly established organization at the University of Tehran that promoted social activities for female students. *(It also encouraged the mingling and socializing between male and female students.)*

While I was studying as an undergraduate, I obtained a part-time job with the American Friends of the Middle East (AFME), an educational organization in Tehran *(The headquarters of this organization was in Washington, D.C., and I believe today it is called AMIDEAST.)* It turned into a full-time position when I graduated from the University of Tehran. *(I was hired as an assistant to the educational counselor.)*

In the fall of 1965, a foreign admissions counselor from Columbia University came to Iran under the auspices of the AFME to study the Iranian educational system *(Joel B. Slocum was his name.)* I was assigned as the interpreter of interviews between the admissions counselor and the Iranian educators and administrators. I was also the translator of the documents that he collected for his study. The result of this research was published by the American Association of Collegiate Registrars and

Admissions Officers in their 1970 World Education Series.

A counseling seminar in May of 1966 gave me the opportunity to join other counselors from AFME's overseas offices in Amman, Jordan where we discussed, exchanged views, and tried to find solutions to the educational problems of Middle Eastern students in the United States.

In September of 1965 I got married. My husband, a geologist, was working for the National Iranian Oil Company. While working at AFME, I continued with my education and completed the MA program in English by the end of May 1968.

My husband accepted a departmental fellowship offered by the geology department at Northwestern University, Evanston, and in mid-June 1968, we both left Iran and came to the United States. He became a full-time graduate student, and I became a full-time mother and a part-time secretary in the geography department at Northwestern.

In 1972, the National College of Education *(today known as National Louis University)* offered me a tuition scholarship to pursue a master's in education. I wrote my thesis on the role of guidance counselors in Iranian secondary schools. While enrolled as a full-time graduate student, I kept my part-time job at Northwestern and accepted the additional work duties required of students who were awarded tuition fellowship. *(Why am I sharing this information? My motivation was probably to let them know I could handle several jobs at the same time!)*

In July of 1973, my husband was employed by AMAX Coal Company in Indianapolis to head the department of planning analysis and evaluation. We moved to Carmel, Indiana.

In the fall of 1975, I began a volunteer program at Carmel Junior

High School that turned into a federally funded project. I planned and organized an effective educational program for the Vietnamese students *(children of the Vietnamese refugees and the boat people who were sponsored by the area churches)* and developed individualized instructions for each of my students. The project lasted two years, at the end of which I published an article about the program in the *Hoosier Schoolmaster.* WNON radio station interviewed me on a program called *Zionsville, USA.* In that hour-long interview, I talked about the ESL program I set up and my work with the Vietnamese children and what we had accomplished.

Upon completion of the above ESL program, I shifted my focus to teaching English to native speakers. In order to do that, I had to get a teaching certificate. As a requirement for the certificate, I was to do one semester of student teaching. I taught ninth grade English, and it was a smashing success. Students were interested and attentive. *(I wonder if they paid more attention because of my accent!)*

I spent many hours preparing materials and organizing activities that were unique. I demanded much, and my students worked hard. Once I assigned a research project to my ninth graders who thought it was too difficult and could not be done. But they all did their share of the research and completed the project and submitted the written report on schedule. The day oral reports were due, I asked the chair of the English department to be present in my classroom. *(Was I trying to impress and show off?)* Later, the principal of the school congratulated me on the fine job my students had done, and the news got around. I believed in the capabilities of my students—probably more than they believed themselves.

On several occasions, school administrators approached me for a full-time teaching position in that school. But at the end of the semester, I had made up my mind that I was not going to pursue a teaching career. *(Amazing to look back at this autobiography because I ended up teaching college-level students and enjoyed it immensely.)*

For three years, I worked on the Parent Advisory Committee of the Reading Clinic in Carmel, Indiana. I edited a special handbook that was given out by the clinic to parents whose children had reading difficulties.

I'm now ready to begin a career of my own *(I suppose that was the reason I was applying to law school. I had decided not to be a teacher then.)* I know I have done a lot so far, but that is not enough. I feel that I have potentials and capabilities that have not been tapped yet due to circumstances and/or responsibilities that have barred me from going ahead full blast. *(Geez, did I write this in 1979? Many years later, I realized why I was feeling unsettled.)*

I hope this short autobiography gives you an idea of the type of person I am *(I would've loved to know what they thought after reading this —oh, I know, I was not granted admission!)* It does not agree with my ingrained modesty *(Oh, really?)*, but I will go ahead and say it: I believe I am unique because I am educated, intelligent, and have a good sense of humor. I am self-confident and exercise common sense. I'm self-motivated and persistent, and I have deep compassion for mankind. Coming from the East and making my home in the West, I have tried to combine the best of the two cultures—that is what I call unique.

This is what I wrote in 1979, verbatim. It said nothing about why I wanted to go to law school, or what had triggered such a desire! In hindsight, I can truthfully say I wanted to do something challenging. I didn't want to teach and I didn't want to stay at home either. So, I thought the next best thing would be to go back to school.

As a kid, I was told not to boast or "toot my own horn." It was not accepted in my family. One had to exercise modesty and humility. "Let others discover your talents and qualities," my parents repeated. After living for a decade in the United States and observing the differences between the two cultures, I realized self-promotion was not only accepted but maybe encouraged! Oh, well, the rest is history!

1

Final Semester at the University of Tehran

Sometimes the line between legal and ethical behavior is blurred.

I think of us as the "four musketeers,"—Mim, Dee, Nan, and I. We have studied a year in the United States and are now completing our undergraduate studies in English at the University of Tehran. It is the end of the semester and the final year of college. Within a month exams will begin, and then we will officially graduate.

It has been an interesting semester. Dee is my closest friend. She and the other two musketeers take French as an elective, but I have opted for German.

Dee confides in me that she is somewhat smitten by her bachelor French professor! Then by mid-semester, she says the professor's mother has visited her family several times.

"What for?" I ask.

"Well, you know! She brought a marriage proposal on behalf of her son."

"Really?" I'm a bit surprised. Although huge age differences in Iranian marriages are considered normal, this professor is at least eighteen years older than Dee, if not more!

The professor is a dashing bachelor, close to forty years old. He has a doctorate, has studied in France, and dresses impeccably—tailored suits, expensive-looking ties with matching pocket kerchiefs.

A couple of times, while waiting for Dee, I peek into the classroom where he is lecturing. I am amazed at how tense the other three musketeers look. Their faces are flushed, and with their eyes transfixed on the bachelor professor, they are feverishly scribbling in their notebooks. He moves from the podium to write something on the board and continues walking back and forth. I chuckle because these girls appear mesmerized. It looks to me as if he has hypnotized these young women by his professional power!

Dee confides again and tells me the details of the professor's mother's visits to their house. Dee's father is alarmed and disapproves of him as an appropriate suitor for his daughter. There is a huge age difference. Yet, Dee is dizzy with excitement. After all, out of all these girls, the professor has chosen her!

Her parents have not responded favorably to the professor's proposal, and the talk about the *mehrieh* has come to a standstill. Traditionally, the *mehrieh* is the sum a groom agrees to pay the bride in case of divorce. It varies from family to family. Dee says her parents are demanding a high *mehrieh*. She is stressed out.

But the story continues!

I hear through the grapevine that another girl in that French class gets calls from this bachelor professor just to chat. She happens to be another one of our musketeers, Mim!

It is spring time in Tehran, and in a month or so, the finals will begin, and by June we will graduate. Dee whispers more details.

"His mother is such a pompous . . . She thinks she is doing me a favor! She sits on the sofa in our living room, crosses her legs, and conducts marriage negotiations on behalf of her son."

Dee's father, a man of letters, well-known and respected in the literary circles, has a calm disposition. However, in this instance he has put his foot down and demands a very high *mehrieh* for his daughter.

It is now March 21, the Persian New Year, and we are off for ten days. During this time, I do not see or talk to Dee because we are out of town on vacation.

When we go back to school, my third musketeer friend, Nan, pulls me aside: "Dee has gone on a hiking trip and has sprained her ankle and can't attend class." Immediately, I know this is an excuse; something has happened.

I call her up. She is distraught and almost crying on the phone. The marriage negotiations were broken off completely, and she doesn't want to attend class for the rest of the semester. There's not much left anyway.

When I see Mim again, she is beaming from ear to ear. Though she does not tell us directly, the news spreads that she is getting married very soon, before the semester ends.

Not too long after, the religious ceremony quickly takes place at her house, they tie the knots, and she is officially the wife of her French professor!

My reaction to this turn of events is rather ambivalent. I'm happy for Mim because that is what she wants. I'm rather sad for Dee because of the emotional roller-coaster she was put through, and I feel angry toward the professor. How could a mature man, in his position, play with the emotional feelings and affections of two young female students simultaneously? Although whatever he did was legal, it certainly was not ethical. That is my opinion.

2

Letter of Recommendation

Sometimes we have to accept bitter disappointment!

Throughout my life, I've been given letters of recommendation for various reasons, like applying to a college, or a job. I have also written letters of reference for my students, whenever they asked me to do so.

But once, I was denied a letter of reference. That was not only a surprise, it also hurt my feelings deeply. I was both mad and sad.

In my final year of high school in Tehran, I participated in an international competition for a scholarship to study a year in the United States. I was selected and received the scholarship. The competition was stiff. It was quite an achievement. A women's magazine in Tehran, *Ettelaat-e Banuvan,* even wrote an article about me. At the time, I was seventeen years old and attending the prestigious, all female high school, *Anoushirvan Dadgar.* Our principal, a short and always elegantly-dressed woman, was the widow of a well-known navy admiral who had passed away several years earlier.

Upon completing my year in the United States, I returned to Iran and was promptly accepted into the department of foreign languages at the University of Tehran.

In my final year of college, the department chair, Dr. Suratgar, suggested I apply for an academic scholarship to a specific college in England. His wife, who was from England, was my advisor on the senior project. They both wrote glowing letters of recommendation on my behalf. I needed a third letter. I thought what better person than the principal of my former high school who was very familiar with my character and academic work.

The day I visited her in her office is still vivid in my mind—even after all these years!

She responded to my enthusiastic hello with lukewarm greetings. I thought she would be proud of my accomplishments since high school graduation. But upon hearing my request for a letter of recommendation for a college scholarship in England, she arched her eyebrows, hemmed and hawed, shifted in her big office chair, and finally said, "It has been a few years since you left this school, I wouldn't know how much you have changed!" She flatly refused to write the reference letter. My jaw fell in disbelief. I had just shared with her my achievements since high school, including getting into the University of Tehran, which was no small feat at the time.

Feelings of anger and sadness flooded my heart. How could she dare to say such words when I had just given her the whole account of my life since high school? The assistant principal, who was also present in the room and knew me well, threw a surprising glance at the direction of her boss. I was on the verge of crying, which would have been embarrassing for a poised twenty-two-year-old. I gently thanked her and left the school. I regretted having asked her.

After college graduation, under circumstances I don't precisely recall, I met a young woman at an organizational meeting. She was about my age. She was pleasant, and we chatted for some time. She mentioned she had also applied, years earlier, for the same international scholarship to study in the U.S., but her application was rejected. We then talked about our former high schools. That is when she casually mentioned her mother was the principal of the high school I attended.

The denied letter of recommendation made a lot more sense to me then! I could only smile.

3

One Summer in My Life

The summer a new chapter opened in my life.

June of 1968 was a tumultuous time in the history of the United States. Martin Luther King Jr. and Bobby Kennedy had been assassinated. College students were rioting against the Vietnam War, and most university campuses were in chaos and disarray. I was twenty-five years old and pregnant with my first child.

When my husband, Khosrow, told one of his friends that we were leaving Iran to continue our education in the U.S., his friend shook his head in disbelief.

"Let me get this straight. You don't speak English, your wife is six months pregnant, you have only $600, and you want to leave your home to go to a country that is in the middle of civil unrest? Buddy, have you had your head examined?"

But that really was our goal, crazy or not. My husband was to attend an intensive English program at Iowa State University during that summer, and then a graduate program at Northwestern University in Evanston, Illinois, in the fall. We both had completed master's degrees at the University of Tehran—his field was geological sciences, and I was an English major. That was us in a nutshell.

Pan American Airlines brought us to O'Hare International Airport in Chicago in the early afternoon hours of June 16, 1968. We had several hours of layover in Chicago before flying to Ames, Iowa.

The word *"Chicago"* sent chills up our spine. We had heard so much about Al Capone and the Mafia. We had watched *The Untouchables* television shows and knew all about the crime in that city. We did not dare to walk out of the terminal.

Finally, getting tired of sitting for hours, I summoned my courage and decided to walk outside. We both walked up and down in front of the terminal, watching for anybody who looked suspicious. After all, we had $600 in cash in a money holder which was hanging around Khosrow's neck, under his shirt. We opted not to risk it and went back inside until it was time for us to board the small commuter plane to Ames.

Flying on a low-altitude commuter plane that held fewer than fifteen people was an unforgettable experience. I could hear the loud noise from the engine propeller, and looking out the window, I could see the green fields and the cows below.

I was wearing a light-green maternity dress with white lace collar that my mother had made. I had short black hair at the time—the officers at O'Hare kept asking if I was from Italy. If I had been relaxed and playful at the time, I could have pretended to be from Sicily, which would have made me feel less anxious about the possibility of the Mafia being at the airport.

It was late in the evening when we landed in Ames, and two ESL instructors were at the airport to greet us. We were to spend the night at Friley Hall—a dorm for young men that had a couple of guest rooms at the very end of the first floor for temporary visitors. The guest room had a bed, a private shower, and a toilet, and it cost $6 per night.

We settled in by 11:00 p.m. and promptly tried to find a place to eat. Across from Friley Hall, I had spotted a McDonald's. Having lived in the U.S. as an exchange student five years earlier, I was eager to introduce the legendary fast-food hamburger and fries to Khosrow. We crossed the street, still wearing our nice clothes (people used to dress up for international air travel over fifty years ago). He was still wearing his suit and tie. As soon as we walked in, young university students stared at us. They were all in hippie-type clothing—the fashion at the time!

The following morning, my husband was off to register for his English classes, and I sat on the bed thinking about what I had to do. The first order of business was to find an apartment. We could not stay at the dorm longer than a couple of nights. I also needed to find an obstetrician.

I walked over to the housing office and had a delightful conversation with the secretary.

"Your husband will be assigned a 'host family' for the duration of his ESL program," she said.

"That is wonderful news."

"We do this for all the foreign students who are learning English so they can experience American family life, eat some home-cooked meals and learn the language at the same time."

Having the first college cafeteria meal—lunch—was an eye-opening experience for Khosrow. He did not care for the food, there was no bread served with the meal, and the portions were too small. We were used to having our main meal at noon, and flat bread was a staple at every meal.

While he was taking the placement tests to determine his level of competency in English, I walked over to the foreign student office to get more information.

They told me my husband was assigned a host family: Mr. and Mrs. Ray Fisher. Mr. Fisher was a scientist and a faculty member at Iowa State. Mrs. Fisher was a full-time mother of four children.

I came back to the dorm and called Mrs. Fisher.

"Hello!" a sweet voice answered.

"My name is Manijeh. My husband is a student here to learn English, and I believe you are his host family." That was our first introduction.

Mrs. Fisher said she would look at the apartment ads in the paper to locate a few places to look at before she came to pick me up the next day. We were to go apartment hunting together.

The next morning, I stood in front of Friley Hall at 9:00 a.m. wearing an off-white maternity dress my mother had made (Mother made all my clothes). It buttoned half way in the middle of the bodice. She had even made the buttons herself. I loved that dress because I thought I looked good in it. I stood at the curb waiting for Mrs. Fisher to arrive.

A car pulled up in front of me. There she was, a beautiful woman with short sandy-brown hair, blue eyes, and a huge smile. She was probably in her late thirties or early forties. She invited me to get in. There was an open newspaper by her side. She had circled a few ads for apartment rentals. *Thank God I could communicate in English, and had no problem meeting new people.*

The places we checked, based on the ads, were not suitable at all for a pregnant woman. They mostly fit the life style of a single undergraduate student. There was one that I remember vividly: a gloomy and dark basement apartment with a tub in the bathroom. Mrs. Fisher commented that stepping in and out of the tub might be difficult for me. The landlady looked me straight in the eyes and said, "Honey, lots of things are difficult when you are pregnant."

We spent another night at Friley Hall. The next morning Khosrow was out early attending his English classes. I sat there on the bed wondering what on earth I was doing there, thousands of miles away from home, sitting alone in a tiny room, pregnant, not knowing what the future held for us.

All I knew was the immediate future. Khosrow had to learn English and pass the TOEFL (Test of English as a Foreign Language) exam in order to make his acceptance to Northwestern University unconditional. Our future depended on his success. My task was to find an apartment and an obstetrician. I did not have much time to wallow in my sorrow. The phone rang and it was Mrs. Fisher.

"I just saw an ad for a sublet apartment on Lincoln Highway. Do you want to go see it?"

"What is a sublet?"

"Oh, the person who has rented the apartment is away for a couple of months, but wants somebody else to use the place and pay the rent."

"Sure! I'll wait out front."

The apartment complex was on Lincoln Highway, a busy and noisy street. But we were not concerned. We had come from Tehran, a huge city with lots of traffic and noise. The original renter had left just about everything in the apartment, including kitchen items. For some reason, the half-full bottle of oil and the salt shaker made an impression on me! I agreed to rent the place, which was on the first floor, and paid the deposit the manager required. It was not an ideal place, but it was certainly better than one room at the end of a dormitory!

We went back to the dorm to fetch our two suitcases, which contained mostly our clothes, some books, and a few baby items that my mother had purchased in the last minute before I left.

Mrs. Fisher asked us to eat dinner with them that evening and meet their children.

When I entered her kitchen, the aroma of golden fried chicken and the sizzling sound in the electric skillet made me, a hungry, pregnant woman, salivate. We had plenty of mashed potatoes, fried chicken, and green beans. Mrs. Fisher had made fruit salad, which she served in individual bowls in front of each plate. The children were gracious, friendly, and curious to meet this young couple from "I-Ran."

Patti, their daughter, with almost platinum blonde hair and blue eyes, was a high school junior. She had the sweetest laugh and giggled often. Mark was tall, thin, and blonde. He was the gentlest and kindest ninth-grader anyone could ever meet. Steve, a good-looking seventh grader with big blue eyes, was the youngest. I also learned their oldest son, Bill, had already graduated from high school and had joined the air force.

I love fried chicken, so I ate a lot that night! My husband who was not too fond of fresh fruit at the time, ate only a bit of his fruit salad. The rest remained in his bowl. I knew it would probably be thrown away, but I was too polite, or shy, to ask for the remainder of his fruit salad. I still regret not having finished it off!

We had no sheets or blankets, but the Fishers brought all that we needed from their home, and, actually, the two of them helped us make our bed in the apartment that evening.

The following day, Khosrow left for his English classes, and I started thinking about dinner and food shopping. There was a Hy-Vee store across the Lincoln Highway.

When I entered the store, I had absolutely no idea what to buy. I lingered in front of the meat counter for about ten minutes looking at different cuts of meat. What was I supposed to do with them?

Frankly, up to that point I had not done any cooking. Back in Iran, I worked full-time at a non-profit organization, and my last position was assistant to the educational counselor. We helped Iranian students with their applications and paperwork for colleges and universities in the United States. American Friends of the Middle East (AFME) had its headquarters in Washington, D.C., and satellite offices in Middle Eastern countries. Besides my full-time job, I was taking a full load of courses for a master's degree; therefore, I never did any cooking. We ate at my parents' house!

While I was contemplating what to do, a woman walked up to the counter and asked the butcher for what she wanted. I glanced at her and innocently asked, "What do you think I should buy?"

She looked at me rather bewildered and then examined my maternity dress, big belly, smile, and accent. She smiled back and replied, "What do you want to fix?"

"I have no idea. Actually, I have never cooked."

She began chuckling and called the butcher back.

"We have a newlywed here, and she needs help with cooking something for dinner." I felt totally embarrassed, and I blushed because I couldn't be a newlywed with that protruding belly! It just wasn't accepted in those days!

The man behind the counter smiled broadly and suggested different cuts of meat, none of which made any sense to me. Finally, he suggested I buy some ground beef and make meatloaf or hamburgers. That, I could do. I thanked them both and moved on.

My next stop was at the butter/margarine section. Another major dilemma—which brand to buy? I counted twenty different types of butter and margarine on display. Which one was I to choose? Back at home, at Ali Agha's corner store, there was only one kind of butter. I didn't know anything about margarine. So, I lingered there for another ten minutes, examining labels and containers. Then a gentleman dashed and passed by me, picked up a brand quickly and turned around to leave.

Without hesitation, I touched his arm, actually almost grabbled it. He stopped, turned, and looked at me.

"Why did you choose that?" I asked with a smile. My innocent question combined with the accent, softened his demeanor and he quickly responded.

"My family likes the taste. Besides, it is cheaper."

Aha! I became aware that in a country with variety of products, people have the option to choose what they liked! But that freedom of choice had to be based on some kind of standard. In this case, the criteria were taste and price. Suffice to say that for the next ten years I continued buying Blue Bonnet margarine!

Little did I know that choosing a certain cut of meat, and deciding on a brand of margarine were easy decisions compared to the choices I would have to make in the future about life, family, and raising a child in the United States.

We learned about tornadoes, what they were, and what to do in case we heard the warnings. Coming from Iran, we were familiar with earthquakes, but we had never heard of tornadoes. We bought a little radio and listened diligently to the weather reports. My concern and question was, "What if it happened during the night while we were asleep?" Our friends assured us that in that situation, the city would turn the sirens on to warn the people. A few nights later, around midnight, I heard the police siren. It was raining heavily. It must be a tornado warning, I thought. We quickly, dressed and dashed out of the apartment—we needed to find a shelter.

Next to the apartment building was a small parking lot, and I saw a van with two people sitting in it. I thought it must be the city van taking people to a tornado shelter. I could still hear the siren of the police car in the distance. In that torrential rain, with no hesitation, I made a mad dash for the van, opened the door, and got into the back seat, followed by Khosrow. The young lady in the front seat made an objection.

"There is a tornado warning. Is this the car to take us to a safe shelter?" I hastily asked.

The young man behind the wheel looked at me with a half-opened mouth.

"There is no tornado warning, not in this rainy weather," the woman replied.

"But the sirens . . ." I was confused.

"Oh, there was an accident two blocks over, and that's where the police cars were going." The couple must have just come back from a date!

I mumbled some words of apology, and we went back to the apartment. The following night, the rain continued with some gusty winds. We slept through it all, comforted by the thought that if there is rain, there is no danger of tornado! When Khosrow went to school in the morning he learned there had been a severe tornado warning the night before, and all students in the dorms had gone to a shelter. Ignorance is bliss!

Our stay at that sublet apartment on Lincoln Highway was short-lived. A one-room attic apartment became available in a residential area on West Street, closer to the Fishers' house. They knew the owner, Mr. and Mrs. Zeliadt. The problem was the very narrow stairs I had to climb to get to the attic apartment. I didn't mind the climb, but for some reason, the people around me were a bit nervous. We decided to take the apartment anyway to be closer to the Fishers and to get away from the noisy Lincoln Highway.

A new Iranian friend volunteered to drive us along with our suitcases, to the new place. But when we reached the apartment, we saw the Fishers standing in front of the building chatting with the owner.

"Sorry, you cannot move in now."

"Why not? What is wrong?" I asked

"The place is full of cockroaches," Mrs. Fisher announced. "The owner has sprayed the apartment with heavy-duty pest control chemicals. It is not safe for you to inhale the fumes."

The car was diverted to the Fishers' house, where we spent the night. Patti graciously offered us her bedroom, and slept on the sofa in the den. She quietly whispered to me that she loved to sleep in the den because she could watch TV.

II

We became part of the Fisher family. Mrs. Fisher made appointments and took me to an obstetrician. Mr. Fisher loaned Khosrow a bicycle to ride to and from school, and I could walk to their house any time of the day.

They had a huge vegetable garden that summer, and I loved to help harvest cucumbers and green beans. I also watched Mrs. Fisher can vegetables and make pickles. That summer we ate plenty of fresh vegetables. I also learned she was a former beauty queen.

That summer in 1968 I learned a lot about cooking, canning, and managing a household. Looking back, I thank my lucky stars that I had such an excellent role model.

We also shared our culture with the Fishers. Khosrow knew how to make Persian rice with a golden crispy bottom—*tahdig*—which the Fishers loved. And I made my one specialty, cream puffs, on several occasions.

By August, English classes had ended and Khosrow had passed his TOEFL exam. The baby's due date was estimated around the first week in September. We had to make a decision: should I stay in Ames, where I had been examined by a doctor regularly, to have the baby, or should I move to Evanston where I did not know anybody, in my ninth month of pregnancy?

It was a huge dilemma for two reasons. If we decided to stay, we could not stay in the apartment, as the landlady wanted us out of there before the beginning of the fall semester. She knew we would be gone once the baby was born. It was impossible to secure a short-term apartment in a university town. Our only other option was to stay in a hotel, which we absolutely could not afford.

This was a crucial time in our lives. I was distraught and truly didn't know what to do. Many times I thought maybe my parents were right in suggesting I stay in Iran, have the baby, and then join my husband. Good or bad, easy or difficult, I had made up my mind that I wanted to be with my husband through thick and thin—not knowing how thin it could get!

One evening, sitting in the Fishers' living room discussing my options, I broke down and cried. I didn't know what to do.

"The solution is easy. You will move in with us," the Fishers suggested.

For a split second, I stopped crying and looked at them—the children were also present in the living room. This was an option I had not considered or thought about. Their generosity and offer made me cry even harder. It was a done deal as far as they were concerned. They must have talked it over among themselves beforehand.

The children's recreation room was converted into a bedroom for us. They had a tri-level house, and the recreation room was on the lower level, near the laundry room and the garage. A shower and a toilet made it perfectly comfortable. We moved in!

September 1 was our third wedding anniversary. The Fishers made the occasion very special for us: they took us out to lunch in Des Moines and pinned a beautiful corsage on me (Ray Fisher's hobby was growing orchids in their greenhouse).

Khosrow received a formal letter from Northwestern University—he was unconditionally accepted and needed to be on campus no later than September 20. We were now ready for the baby to show up and consulted the doctor about whether induced labor was okay. That was not normally recommended for the first baby, so we decided to wait a little longer.

On September 22, still with no baby in sight, my husband boarded the Greyhound bus for Chicago.

He called the next day to let me know that we had a small, one-bedroom apartment in a university-owned building, Dryden Hall. And I stayed with the Fisher family to have the baby in Ames. What a blessing those days were!

In the midst of anxiety, excitement, and unknowns, we also had loads of fun and plenty of laughter. While expecting the baby's arrival any minute, Mrs. Fisher and I did something fun and unusual. We left the house at six o'clock one morning to attend a special free showing of Doris Day's film *With Six You Get Eggroll*. Continental breakfast was also included. We giggled all the way to the theater, wondering if the neighbors thought we were headed for the hospital.

It was 2:00 a.m. on September 24 that I thought I was having contractions, but I wasn't sure. To be on the safe side, I knocked on the Fishers' bedroom door. By then, I was calling them by their first names, Dottie and Ray.

They got up immediately. With Dottie and I in one car, and Ray escorting us in another, we drove to Mary Greeley Hospital in Ames. Dottie spent the entire night at the hospital with me, while Ray returned home. Despite regular contractions, nothing happened till morning when the doctor broke the amniotic fluid. I gave birth to a baby boy at 3:27 p.m.

That afternoon, I made two phone calls from the hospital to announce the birth of our child. One was to Khosrow in Evanston; the other was to my sister, Jaleh, who was an undergraduate student at Mills College in California. As I learned later, the phone company was on strike in Chicago at the time so Khosrow could not get a phone installed in the apartment right away. The number he had given me was for another tenant in the building.

When my sister heard the news, she cried with joy on the phone. Khosrow's reaction to the news was more interesting! In the midst of the excitement for the birth of his son, he kept saying, "Buy yourself the dress you liked." I had seen a simple brown dress with a "waistline" and had commented that as soon as I gave birth, I was going to wear something like that with a belt! After long hours of labor and delivery with twenty stitches, buying a dress was not on my mind.

I learned a lot during my six-day stay at the hospital. My roommate was a pleasant woman, having her fourth child, and taught me what to order for meals.

"Make sure you get prune juice with every meal," she advised. Not only I had received twenty stitches after my baby's birth, I had also developed hemorrhoids, both were extremely painful. At the hospital, I also learned how to breast feed and put a diaper on the baby.

Ray Fisher had passed out cigars at the university, and Dottie brought homemade coffee cakes and peanut brittle for the nurses. I was a member of their family, like a young sister or a daughter. Khosrow and I had agreed that depending on the gender of the baby, we would use their names as a middle name for our child. Hence our son's name is Kasra Ray.

Kasra and I stayed in Ames till October 18 when the Fishers drove us to Evanston, Illinois, to reunite with my husband. I vividly remember the headlines in the newspaper that morning: "Jackie Kennedy to Marry Aristotle Onassis."

It was almost 7:00 p.m. when Ray parked the car in front of Dryden Hall. Our one-bedroom apartment was on the third floor. They sent me and the baby upstairs to meet Khosrow, so he could see his son for the first time. By then Kasra Ray was twenty-four days old.

My husband opened the door, and I handed him the baby; he smiled from ear to ear.

"But he is so tiny," he said. Months later, when I repeated his comment to a friend, she laughed and said, "What did he expect, a teenager?"

That summer in 1968, we watched societal upheavals, and learned about the presidential elections and the two major political parties in the United States. From the living room of our host family, we watched on television what happened at the Democratic National Convention held in Chicago in August. Although the sight of hippies was new to me, I knew enough not to stare at the young men with long hair and strange clothing.

A lot was going on during that summer, but I was preoccupied with my own immediate concerns: having my first child away from my home and family, trying to immediately secure a place to live in Evanston—after the difficult housing situation we experienced upon arrival in Ames—and being supportive of my husband.

Originally, when we applied to Northwestern for graduate studies, I was granted admission to the counseling program. But when I became pregnant, our plans changed. My goal of getting a doctorate had to be put on the back burner. It was twenty-five years later before I went back to college to accomplish this goal.

On Tuesday, November 5, 1968, in the midst of the Vietnam War, Mr. Nixon was elected president. We knew the Fishers were Republicans, so I called Dottie the next day.

"Congratulations!" I said.

"Congratulations for what, honey?" Dottie asked with her usual sweet voice.

"Well, Mr. Nixon got elected," I explained.

III

That first quarter at Northwestern University was one of the toughest for Khosrow. Not only did he struggle with English and the text-books for various courses, he also had a tough time adjusting to a new life and the culture in America. I had a different type of adjustment of my own to make: learning how to take care of a new baby, with the constant reminder that we were totally on our own to make it in this land of opportunity.

1968 to 1972 was the best of times, and it was the worst of times. We were not the only poor graduate students. We became friends with other graduate students who were in the same financial situation—almost all were on a graduate stipend or part of a fellowship program.

When we got together with other families for potluck dinners, it was fascinating to listen and learn about everyone's research projects—such a smart group of young people all gathered under one roof.

Life in Dryden Hall was fascinating and had its interesting moments. The building was originally a condo-like hotel that was purchased by the university and turned into apartment units for married students. We lived on the third floor at the end of the hall. Directly across from our apartment lived a couple from Israel with their four-year-old daughter, Ronit, who had gorgeous blue eyes. The Hanani became good friends, and we babysat for each other often. Above us, on the fifth floor, lived Michael and Heidi Steinitz with their little boy, Daniel.

Michael's grandmother, whom I met only once when she came for a visit, was a fascinating woman. She had fled Nazi Germany and had brought her family to America. She told the most amazing stories about her struggles to get out of Germany. I recall at one point I got very emotional and cried when she told one of her stories. We made some life-long friends while living in Dryden Hall, many of whom we still talk to, or get together occasionally.

Our friendship with the Fisher family continued, mostly through letters. We did not have the means to make frequent long distance phone calls. The beauty of writing letters is that one can read them over and over again. That is what I did with the letters I received from Dottie, and my own parents who lived across the ocean.

Keeping connected with the people we love takes time and energy. During those years at Northwestern, while Khosrow was studying hard, I felt it was my responsibility to keep his parents, my parents, and the Fishers informed of what was going on in our lives.

As a new mother, I had plenty to learn myself. At that time, *The Common Sense Book of Baby and Child Care* written by Dr. Benjamin Spock was the book everyone consulted. I bought a copy and referred to it on numerous occasions.

We formed a babysitting co-op in Dryden Hall and helped each other. Financial hardship was compensated by the charm of simple friendship and intellectuality. We also pulled our resources together and often arranged pot lucks on weekends. The assortment of food displayed on tiny tables in those small apartments was a sight to behold. From hummus and pita bread and stuffed grape leaves to rice pilaf and succulent lamb stew cooked with vegetables—we had it all even on our shoestring budgets. It was all in the sharing! We laughed and talked about our children; even the husbands shared their departmental gossip, course work and their anxieties about the pressures of graduate school.

Relationship and friendship—that is what life is all about. At any stage of life, when we look back at our ups and downs, trials and errors, happy times and sad times, what we remember the most are the good friends and the fine relationships we have formed with others. For me, it is also the kindness and the unconditional love I received from a family in Ames, Iowa, one summer in my life.

4

Learning to Cook

It took a while, but I finally learned how to cook and bake well.

My mother was a good cook. Now and then I had the opportunity to watch her, but I never actually practiced the art of cooking. My mother never baked. All the sweets we had came from the local pastry shops. Throughout high school and college, I never tried my hands at cooking or baking. The message I got from my mother was, "Concentrate on your studies; you will get your chance to cook and bake later."

But God gave me a sweet tooth and planted in me a deep fondness for pastries and baked goods! I was deprived a cream puff when I was six years old, and the scar remained for years, so I taught myself how to make cream puffs, or eclairs. Once I was able to make those puffs, I made and ate them often. In the summer, I filled them with ice cream, and they tasted heavenly. But still I didn't know how to cook.

I came to the United States when I was seventeen years old and lived with an American family in Ohio. They asked me about Iranian food and whether I could make something for them. I could not. I had eaten my mother's food and could only describe how delicious it was! I must have said something about stuffed green peppers, *dolmeh*, because a week later my American mom prepared the stuffed green pepper dish. Well, she tried to make it. I don't know who gave her the recipe or how she found it, but it did not taste like anything I had eaten before. The green peppers were stuffed with some chopped meat and rice that were not totally cooked or blended with sauce and spices. My other siblings in the family didn't like it either, but everyone was polite, and they forced themselves to eat it. I was torn. While I wanted to appreciate my host mom's effort in making the dish, I also wanted to tell everyone that this was not how *dolmeh* was supposed to taste. But I let it go.

One of the dishes my host mother prepared and I loved was meatloaf. Consequently, when I left the United States and returned to Iran, I was proud and pleased that at least I could make one American dish: meatloaf.

I began my college studies and had a job as well—cooking was out of the picture. Mother prepared the meals, and I gladly ate, whenever I came home from school or work. What a piece of work I must have been! But she did know that I appreciated her cooking.

I got married after graduating from college. It was only logical to inform my husband, Khosrow, that I could make two things: meatloaf and cream puffs. Not bad for a newlywed! He was proud and told his mother. We went to his parents' house so that I could show my culinary expertise to my in-laws and his siblings. Little did I know what loomed ahead!

Not being familiar with my mother-in-law's oven and its temperature setting, the meatloaf took much longer to cook, and when it finally came out of the oven, it didn't taste like what I had eaten in the U.S. His parents and siblings were too polite to say anything, but I bet they promised themselves never to let me get close to the kitchen again! And they never did.

It really was not my fault. The oven temperature was not what I had expected. I am certain of that. How do I know that? Because of the second disaster the same day! Everyone waited patiently for the midafternoon snack—the puffs. We were to fill them with ice cream when they came out of the oven. I had made those puffs many times using my mother's oven. They always came out puffed and golden. But no, not in my in-law's house. When I finally took them out of the oven, they had not puffed and were clumps of cooked dough. Khosrow's nine-year-old brother commented, "These are so hard!" Yes, I agreed; you could break a head with those round, hard, mini bricks!

Khosrow and I came to the U.S. for graduate studies. He told an Iranian classmate that his wife was also Iranian and invited the young man over for a Persian meal. God knows I tried! I made *loobia polo*—a combination of meat, green beans, tomato sauce, and spices mixed with rice and baked. The classmate came over, ate, and at the end commented, "This tastes like something my mother used to make. We called it *loobia polo*," he said, and quickly added, "But it didn't look anything like this."

I jumped up from my chair, unable to hold my tongue and shot back, "What do you think you have been eating? This is *loobia polo*!"

Later, I joined the Dames Club at Northwestern University and met ladies who had cooking experience and shared recipes with me. I even joined the cookbook-of-the-month club and purchased a one-year subscription.

Those days are behind me now, and after fifty-five years of marriage, the cream puffs are still at the top of my list, and our meals are mostly grilled. Thank God, in America, men love their BBQ grill!

5

Citizenship

What does it mean to be an American citizen?

B ack in 1978, when I made a conscious decision to become a U.S. citizen, it was not out of desperation, necessity, or political anxiety. It truly was a decision based on deep emotional soul-searching, understanding, and a strong desire to live and die in the United States of America.

On that October 17, when my husband and I went through the formalities of the swearing-in ceremony in Indianapolis and took the oath of allegiance while our ten-year old son watched, I knew that I had opened a new chapter in my life and that I had made an important decision that would have a significant impact on my life. My loyalty was shifting to a country that I was not born into. Becoming a U.S. citizen came with enormous responsibilities. I took the "Pledge of Allegiance" very seriously, and pondered its every word; I was pledging to the flag and all that it represented.

I left the courthouse and the ceremony with a bundle of books and pamphlets. The right to be a citizen could not be taken lightly. My education and personal journey to citizenry had just started. I learned about the duties of a citizen and the rights and privileges that came with it. Did I have enough time to learn all about the Constitution, the history of this land, and my state and local governments? I opted for a short cut. When I took my ten-year-old to the local library, I utilized the children's section to read quickly and furiously. I figured the historical information and facts were the same, they were just presented in a more simple and easy language.

The words to "The Star-Spangled Banner" were not easy to memorize, but I learned the tune. I once confessed to a friend: "I get a lump in my throat whenever I hear the national anthem." She looked at me with tears in her eyes and said, "That is the way it's supposed to feel." It was comforting to know I was experiencing emotions that were okay.

When my husband's boss learned that we both had become U.S. citizens, he and his wife invited us to a lovely dinner at their home to celebrate. She had little American flags planted in front of our plates. They were proud of us, and it confirmed, once more, that we had made an important decision. During all these events, our son, Kas, remained a silent observer. He was born in Iowa.

It was not until our son was in seventh grade that I realized the impression our change of citizenship had left on him. In an essay competition on Americanism, sponsored by the Elks Lodge in Idaho, he wrote about the American he most admired. He chose his father, and in one part of the essay he wrote, "The day I was in court to witness him take the oath of citizenship is very vivid in my mind and I was so proud." He won the third place and was given a check for $25.00. I kept the stub.

Forty-three years have passed since that day. I have voted in presidential elections, campaigned for local candidates, witnessed profound societal changes, raised a son, lived in different states across this vast nation, and in the process, I've also taught and educated some college students along the way.

When I learned through reading one of my student's journal entry assignments that she had become a U.S. citizen, it was a perfect opportunity to congratulate her publicly in class and let other students ponder the importance of citizenship. I made a big deal about her citizenship, hoping my American-born students would not take their citizenship for granted. Sometimes immigrants appreciate and recognize the privileges of being a U.S. citizen more than those who never have to think about what it truly means.

6

Buying a New House

The agony and ecstasy of buying a new house!

I like our very first house. For a family of three—me, my husband, and our ten-year-old son—it is comfortable and adequate. It has three bedrooms and is within walking distance to a good school (kindergarten through ninth grade). A neighborhood swimming pool, tennis courts, and shopping centers are all close by. It is located on a cul-de-sac, so there is no through traffic. Our backyard is large and pie-shaped, with several trees, and there is a narrow creek that runs at the end of the backyard.

We must be pure nuts to want to sell this house!

The whole saga began right after Thanksgiving when a nice, vivacious real estate lady started coming around with brochures, telling us how much our property had increased in value. She insisted on doing a market evaluation of our property. She even brought us a free poinsettia plant for Christmas!

"What the heck, let her do a market analysis! We don't plan to sell anyway, but we can find out how much our house is worth in today's market." I said to my husband.

After the market evaluation came in, again I said to my husband, "Hey, what can we lose? Let me go around and check other houses and see how much a bigger home costs."

He was not thrilled about the idea, but he didn't object to it either.

So, the realtor—the nice lady who gave us the poinsettia—kept coming over and took me around town. I saw a lot of houses: new ones, previously-owned ones, half-finished ones under construction, the just-finished ones. It was a great educational opportunity. I learned plenty about different builders, their style and quality of work. I increased my vocabulary, as I learned the terminology and lingo used in building and construction. None of the houses I saw appealed to me, so there was no point in even asking my husband to come and see any of them. However, I would report my findings to him.

When the realtor showed me a house, I asked myself, "What does this house have that my own doesn't?"

Aha, my present house did not have a formal dining room or a basement!

With these two rooms on top of my list, the realtor kept showing me houses with basements and formal dining rooms! But none of them felt as nice or as comfortable as my own. We are all partial toward our own home and property, but frankly, no offence to any builder, the new homes did not look as solid or well-built.

My quest for a better-built house took us to a higher price range. Now, I was looking at homes, almost twice the price range I had in mind. Then one day, we came across a house that had been vacant for quite some time—the owners had moved to Arizona. The realtor informed me the house had been on the market for a while because the price was too high. I rather liked it and asked my husband to take a look that same evening. Frankly, he didn't care for it much, but graciously said if I liked it we could go ahead and make an offer. We planned to do so the next day.

The following day, early in the morning, the realtor called to say the house had been sold the night before for the full asking price!

We began our search all over again. This time, I had zeroed in on certain locations—now we had to find a house within a certain price range and within the area of our choice. Obviously, that made it much harder. I was getting discouraged, thinking I'd never find a house that I liked. Then I would remind myself the idea had started leisurely, that we were not serious about selling and moving.

Then, one day in early spring, my neighbor and I went for our morning jog. I noticed she could hardly keep her eyes open. Come to find out, she and her husband had negotiated and bought a house the night before. The offer-and-counter-offer process had dragged on till 3 a.m. After that she had been too excited to fall asleep. Instead of jogging, we got into her car and drove to see the house. All we talked about that morning was houses. I knew that they had been looking, off and on, for a bigger house. I was indeed happy for them.

That afternoon, my realtor picked me up, and on our way to see some more homes, she pointed to a house and said she was going to show it to me, but the house was sold late last night.

"I know. It was sold to my neighbor at 3:00 a.m.," I replied.

Now that my neighbor who happened to be a good friend was moving, I was determined to find a new house and move too!

Lo and behold, a month later, I came across a lovely Dutch colonial-style house. The owners were planning to move to Michigan—a transfer by his company. It had a formal dining room and a partially finished basement! And it was in the neighborhood we wanted. The price was a bit more than what we anticipated. And there was a catch! If we bought the house, we could not move in for three months. They were building a new house in Michigan that was not ready yet.

"So what? We can wait three months. We have a house to sell too!" I said to my husband.

By early fall we moved into the new house. After almost a full year of constant searching, we had finally found what we wanted, and the location was ideal.

Does anyone believe in destiny or kismet? I do.

A month after we moved into the new house, my husband received a call from a company in Boise, Idaho. They wanted him to head a newly established computer department. They made him an offer he could not refuse.

We were out of that dream house right after Thanksgiving!

7

Lost in Translation

Warning: Translating expressions verbatim from one language into another can be hazardous. A friend told me the following story.

A young man from Iran is a college student in the United States. His English is very limited, and he is in the habit of translating expressions in his native tongue into English, which totally changes their meaning. Sometimes the sayings don't make any sense at all.

This young man's buddy, also from Iran, has bought a new car and invites him to go for a ride in it. Somewhere along the way, the driver misses a stop sign. Immediately, a cop pulls them over.

With very limited knowledge of the English language and not knowing the customs of the new country, the two students start trembling. They are scared to death and look it.

"Did you know that you did not stop at the stop sign?" the police officer asks.

With wide eyes and an open mouth, the bewildered driver looks at the cop. His friend in the passenger seat immediately translates an expression from his native tongue that is equivalent to a profound apology and admission of guilt. He stretches his neck toward the officer and apologizes on behalf of the driver, delivering his translated apology: "Officer, he made a mistake. He ate shit!"

The officer, seeing these two trembling young men and hearing that one has eaten shit, thinks they are headed for the hospital. Without further ado, he instructs them to follow him. They obey.

With the officer leading the way, the two students, worried and scared, follow the police car, which stops in front of the emergency area of the local hospital.

On the way there, the cop had radioed the hospital telling them of the emergency situation. So, as soon as they arrive at the hospital, two orderlies show up with a stretcher. They put the driver of the car on the stretcher and rush him inside. His friend runs after them, frazzled and wide-eyed, not knowing what the hell is going on.

Once they get into a room, nurses and doctors rush in to pump the young man's stomach. They try to explain to him what they are about to do.

The young man starts crying and wailing, turning to his friend he says, "In our country, when you have traffic violation, they only give you a ticket. But here in America, they pump your stomach."

Then they both sob!

8

A Teaching Challenge

Once upon a time, I taught English as a second language to Vietnamese and Chinese students in Carmel, Indiana.

The concept of readiness is the most important part of pedagogy. It is also the most sensible approach to teaching anything, and I'm not talking about only academic subjects.

When I taught English as a second language (ESL) to a group of Vietnamese students, I was not formally aware of the concept of readiness, but I knew by instinct that I could not teach them something for which they had absolutely no background information.

Teaching ESL to a group of Chinese and Vietnamese students who did not know a word of English and looked at me with expressionless faces was a challenge. Normally, eyes reveal a lot, so I made sure we made plenty of eye contact. I kept watching for that special spark that would indicate to me that they had reached the "aha" moment.

Readiness for this group of students meant a lot of show-and-tell. To get them ready for a lesson on prepositions, for example, I put a huge box in the middle of the classroom. For one whole period, various objects kept floating in, out, over, under, near, behind, and beside the box. When the time came to read the text and do the exercises, they had a frame of reference. It made it a lot easier for them to use the prepositions correctly.

Then, one day I could no longer use my method of "show-and-tell." When a seventeen-year-old Chinese boy, and a sixteen-year-old Vietnamese girl came to me and asked me to explain what VD meant, I was at a loss.

For two whole days I researched the subject, talked to the health and physical education teacher, consulted with the librarian, and looked through all the available teaching materials, books and filmstrips. Finally, I put together a decent fifteen-minute presentation on venereal disease, in simple words, void of complicated medical terms, given their limited knowledge of the English language.

At the time, my students were of mixed ages. For the younger ones, the presentation would not be appropriate, so I made a special arrangement to present the material to just the two older ones who had asked the question.

They both listened carefully and watched the presentation.

"Now, do you understand what VD is?" I asked to make sure there were no ambiguities.

Then my Chinese student raised his hand and in broken English announced:

"Yes, Teacher, my friends already told me. It is Valentine's Day!"

It was indeed the middle of February, and the letters VD were on display in bright red all over the school.

9

Saving a Marriage

I'm not a marriage counselor,
but I've sometimes been asked to meddle!

I was having lunch at a family restaurant when a gentleman friend approached my table. He delivered the usual pleasantries quickly and then plunged into his request.

"Could you talk to my wife? I'm having some difficulties at home, and it would be good for her to talk to someone like you and ask for advice."

My first reaction was to ask about the nature of the problem. I'd known the couple for many years. On the surface, everything looked fine, and I was not aware of any problem between them. He hemmed and hawed and did not give me a straight answer. I told him I would call and talk to his wife.

They had a nice house on several acres of land. They were well-off as he had a successful business. She was an immaculate housekeeper and a fabulous cook. They had a two-year-old son, and the husband's elderly mother lived with them. The wife did the laundry, the ironing, and took care of the yard, as well as the quails and the chickens they were raising. She appeared to have a cordial and warm relationship with her mother-in-law. What was this man's problem? Could it be bedroom issues? I was puzzled.

I met with her several times. At one point, I loaned her a small booklet on intimacy, which I did not get back! After many conversations and by digging deeper, I eventually learned her husband was pressuring her to get out and get a job.

It didn't make sense for two major reasons: they didn't need the money, and by staying at home, she was saving him a ton of money! It was time to sit down with both of them.

I made a list of everything she did and assigned monetary value to all her services. I put down in writing what it would cost him to pay for a cleaning lady, elder care, childcare, laundry services, a cook, and a gardener. Our country's GNP, unfortunately, does not take into account the services produced by housewives. Sad, but true!

When I presented him with the list of what her services would be worth in actual dollar amount, compared to what she would be making if she got a job outside of the house, he clearly saw the picture. But he was still unhappy! The real reason, I found out, was that he wanted her to get out of the house to do something different and become a more interesting person!

Aha! That is when I thought of our local library.

At the time, I was the president of the Friends of our local library, and I worked closely with the staff and the library director on some fundraising projects. I explained the situation to the director and asked if it were possible to offer the young woman a non-paying "job." We didn't want it to be called "volunteering." She had to have a "job" to go to. We set it up for two days a week where she would work at the library, and those days coincided with the days the library offered programs for children—she was able to take her son with her! I advised this young woman that under no circumstance was she to miss "work" or be absent from her "job."

The rest is history. She got out of the house two days a week, became friends with other ladies at the library, learned a lot about what was going on in the community, and improved her knowledge of current events, and her child attended some quality story times.

People usually don't think of a library as a marriage saver. In this case it was!

10

A Defining Moment

Out of sheer ignorance, I unknowingly created embarrassing situations for my son when he was a teenager. Parenting is not easy!

Silly me, I was insanely excited when my son, Kas, attended his first school dance in eighth grade. It was the beginning of his teen years, and all the social activities associated with it. Of course, he could not drive at the time. We, the parents, decided to carpool. One parent volunteered to drive the boys to the dance. My husband and I offered to pick them up afterward.

It was eleven o'clock in the evening when we pulled in front of the junior high school. The dance was over and all the students were outside in front of the building, laughing, talking, and waiting for their rides.

Like a total idiot, in my excited state of mind, I jumped out of the car, smiling from ear to ear, and began looking for Kas in the midst of the crowd. Today, I can justify my foolish behavior and blame it on not having been raised in the United States and not being familiar with junior high school etiquette. But I didn't know I was doing anything wrong then.

I unwittingly committed the ultimate sin by opening my mouth. Smiling broadly, I asked a couple of young boys, "Did you folks have a good time?" They pretended not to hear me, turned their backs, and walked away. It was as if I were the personification of some kind of nasty disease that they wanted to get away from as quickly as possible.

After a few seconds, I spotted my son and his friends. To my amazement, he treated me like a total stranger. Without saying a word, he quickly climbed into the back seat of the car. His friends climbed in—not a word from any of them. That is when I sensed something was really wrong, but I didn't know what it was!

I quietly slipped into the front seat next to my husband. *What had gone wrong?* My greatest wish was for them to have a good time, but now they sat somberly in silence.

My husband tried to crack a few jokes. But no one responded. We dropped off the boys who had continued holding on to their code of silence. My brain began searching for clues. *What could have possibly gone wrong at the dance?*

We had house guests at the time, and they were still up chatting in the living room when we arrived. My son headed directly to his room. I was left standing and thinking of possible scenarios.

After a few minutes, he came down and with an authoritative voice said, "Mom, may I speak with you?"

Bewildered, with a tinge of curiosity and anxiety, I replied, "Sure, what is it?"

I followed him directly to the laundry room, and he closed the door for privacy.

With an adult-like tone of voice, he informed me of my inappropriate behavior. What I had done was a huge "no-no" in the eyes of junior high school students: I had committed a sin by getting out of the car, and, worse yet, by speaking to the students.

"No parent does that," he said. "It is not acceptable behavior."

I gawked at him, my mouth agape. Finally, when he was finished, I simply apologized and hastily mumbled something to the effect that my behavior was due to cultural differences and my lack of understanding of the accepted social norms. I had no intention of embarrassing him in front of his friends. He accepted my apology, and we dropped the subject.

I never showed my face around his school again, and if I did, I was incognito!

Ten years passed. My husband and I visited Kas at the University of Washington where he was a medical student. Over lunch, he turned to me with a smile and asked, "Mom, do you remember our conversation in the laundry room after the school dance?"

I nodded. How could I ever forget the lecture I received that evening behind closed doors? He chuckled and said that my apology that evening was the turning point in our relationship. He had appreciated the fact that I accepted his criticism graciously.

I never knew that my sincere and simple apology had made such an impact. It was definitely a defining moment in a mother and son's relationship.

11

Making a Transition

I knew it was time to delve into something more challenging!

In early spring of 1983, I announced to my husband, "I want to get a job," and hastily added, "Outside of the house!"

"What do you want to do?" he casually asked while eating his breakfast.

"I'm not sure yet, but it won't be teaching. I'm certain of that." I definitely wasn't planning to apply for teaching jobs.

We had moved from Indiana to Boise, Idaho in 1980, for the usual job opportunities that take one's husband from one state to another. While in Indiana, I had completed all the requirements for a secondary teaching certificate, and I had student-taught at a local junior high school. Though I had enjoyed my experiences as a student-teacher and the interactions with my colleagues were most pleasant, dealing with budding adolescents was not. One day cute and nice, another day obnoxious and belligerent—the Jekyll and Hyde type—they were not exactly my cup of tea! So, when the principal offered me a teaching position after I was done with the requirements for certification, I did not take it, and then we moved to Idaho.

In Idaho, I became a stay-at-home mother for a few years so I could get used to Boise, and find my way around. I volunteered at my son's elementary school, got to know other parents, and made good friends. Now I was ready to do something else with my time. I wanted to get a real job, somewhere outside of the house.

We had opened a savings account with a local brokerage firm in town, and I had visited the office on numerous occasions. Frankly, the world of investments and stocks and bonds was foreign to me. The sight and sound of the electronic ticker tape above the cashier's window, where I deposited checks, was a novelty. I saw people who just sat in the waiting area, almost motionless, with their eyes glued to the fast-moving symbols and numbers on that electronic tape. On those occasional visits, I also noticed men and women—mostly men—sitting at their desks in cubicles and talking on the phone constantly. I had no idea what they were saying. But it all seemed fast-paced. *Wouldn't it be fun to try my hand at a job like this?* It would be totally different from dealing with teenage students, and I could learn something new.

Next time that Jeff, the financial advisor who handled our account, called I was ready to ask some questions. He was an interesting fellow with a PhD in literature and linguistics. For reasons of his own, he had opted to enter the world of finance and the stock market. Short and trim, with sandy-colored hair and round wire-rimmed glasses, he looked like the pictures of James Joyce I had seen in books! Invariably, he opened his calls by commenting on British authors. We would discuss James Joyce, Graham Greene—he knew my master's dissertation was on Graham Greene—and his favorite, Joseph Conrad's *Heart of Darkness*. So we always had a pleasant literary discussion at the beginning of his phone calls before he delved into pitching his side of the deal commenting on our brokerage account and making suggestions and recommendations for our portfolio.

As an English major, with a couple of master's degrees (MA and MEd), I thought maybe I could do something in that firm, despite my lack of knowledge about the stock market and the world of finance.

"So, what other positions are available at this office besides what you do?" I asked casually.

"Oh, we have sales assistant positions—SA for short. They handle clients' accounts, help the brokers, answer the phones, and research and solve problems when needed. In short, they are liaisons between the brokers, clients, and the operation folks in the firm," he explained.

"Sounds interesting and challenging! Any openings for such a position?" I asked nonchalantly.

"I don't know, but why don't you make an application? I'm sure there will be openings in the future as there is always a turnover, SAs come and go." He gave a chuckle.

We left it at that, and another year passed by. By then, we had adjusted to life in Boise and made friends, my son was already in junior high school, and my husband was enjoying his new job at the corporate office in Boise. It was time for me to take serious action and enter the work force.

So, in May of 1983, with my resume in hand, I walked into the office of that brokerage firm for an interview. I was glad my own financial consultant was on vacation—he would not know of my attempt, if the interview was a flop! I had no sales background whatsoever, but I calmed myself down by remembering that once upon a time I had sold Avon products from a catalog to ladies in our student housing apartment at Northwestern University—that was eons ago! Although I didn't mention it on my resume, it boosted my self-confidence when it came to "sales experience!"

I had an appointment to meet with the office manager's assistant, Althea. Despite my punctuality, she let me sit in the waiting area for about half an hour. A good opportunity indeed to watch the floor, hear the constant ringing of the phones and the noise of the ticker tape, observe the scurrying sales assistants running orders to the wire operator, and watch the comings and goings of the employees and the clients. *How exciting! I already like the energy and the dynamics of this place!*

By the time the interview was over, I learned the only position for someone like me was indeed the sales assistant job: answering phones, supporting the brokers, completing paperwork for new clients to open an account, and trouble-shooting when there was a problem with clients' accounts. The job required good communication skills, agility, and calmness under pressure. *I'm sure I can handle the job!*

"Unfortunately, we do not have any openings for a new sales assistant," said the interviewer, interrupting my thoughts. "However, we have created a new position for a receptionist. Would you like to be considered for that?" she asked. *A receptionist! Hmm—why not? One has to start somewhere!*

"Yes, that would be fine with me." I said without hesitation, although I had no idea what I was supposed to do as a receptionist in that firm.

"We want you to take a little entrance test called FIAT. It is a financial aptitude test. Nothing elaborate. It just deals with numbers and fractions," she said.

Gee-whiz! When was the last time I took a math class?

"That would be fine," I said with a smile. "Do you want me to take it right now?"

Althea picked up a booklet from the bottom drawer of her desk and a pencil with an eraser at the end—I looked to make sure it had one! We walked to the lower level of the building, entered a quiet, small room with a couple of desks and few chairs scattered around. The room was secluded with no windows. Sitting at one of the desks was a tall, good-looking gentleman with a mass of dark curly hair—he had a whole bunch of books sprawled in front of him. Obviously, he was studying for something. He looked familiar, but I could not place where I had seen this gentleman. Several days later, however, it dawned on me that he was the former basketball coach at Boise State University, and I had seen his picture in the paper. *What was he studying?*

"Hi, Dave! This lady will be taking the FIAT test down here. I hope you don't mind," the manager's assistant explained.

"Not at all. Please . . ." he said and went right back to reading his books.

The test was not timed, but one had to answer the questions within a reasonable time frame. It was a math aptitude test, no calculators allowed.

Two days later, I received a call and was offered the receptionist position, and I began working on May 20, 1983. It was the beginning of a new chapter in my life.

12

Office Mail

When I was forty years old, I got a job at a well-known brokerage firm in Idaho.

The fascinating world of stocks, bonds, mutual funds, insurance, and money was a far cry from my degree in teaching English. I loved my new job because it was exciting and challenging, and I learned something new every day. During my first year at that brokerage firm, my learning curve was so steep that I'd have lost my hat if I had looked up!

I didn't just have to learn about buying and selling stocks, and dealing with clients' accounts. I also had to learn the rules and regulations that prevailed in that line of business. They called it "compliance." One had to comply with the rules set by the firm or the industry. If not, one had to deal with the compliance manager, who carried with him the aura of a serious and scary assistant principal in charge of discipline.

Each profession has its lingo, and one must learn the terminology.

There are also professional rules and etiquette for how to communicate to clients, how to ask questions, and what information to put down, or not put down, in writing.

Daily market fluctuation was the exciting part. One never knew what the market would do in the course of the day. We had a small electronic ticker-tape on the wall, right above the cashier's window, where clients deposited or picked up checks. The ticker tape showed the stock symbol of each company and whether the price was up or down. It clicked and ticked as long as the stock market was open. Sometimes, retired folks came in and sat on the comfortable sofa in the reception area and intently watched this fast-moving electronic tape, as if their eyes were glued to this device with its constant ticking noise.

Our operations area was for solving clients' problems or catching errors on customers' financial statements. Clients were not allowed in the operations area, but I could go there to ask questions of the bookkeeping crew.

Housed in the operations area was the cashier's section. The head cashier was a woman named Jane, a nice, matter-of-fact, tough lady who rode her motorcycle every day to the office. Whenever I was in the back room waiting for a problem to be solved by one of the bookkeepers, Jane and I would engage in small talk.

Jane was in charge of opening all the incoming mail. Clients would send in checks, documents, or notes and letters to their financial advisors—she opened them all and then distributed the mail to the appropriate recipients. If she saw anything out of the ordinary, the compliance manager would be informed.

After about six months in that firm, I saw Jane approaching my desk, right after lunch, holding a small padded manila envelope. My heart started beating fast. But she had a smile on her face, so I did not panic but relaxed and felt comfortable that it was not a compliance issue!

She came closer, bent her head and handed me the envelope. While chuckling, she said, "Glad I'm the one who opens the mail—no one else has seen it."

I looked at the return address on the envelope. It was from a dear friend in Ohio. What could it be? And why did she send me something to the office address?

With Jane still standing there, I took the envelope and gingerly opened it under my desk. It contained a black-and-white lacy G-string and a couple of pairs of sheer Halloween stockings! The card said, "Trick or Treat. Inside, she wrote, "I was too embarrassed to send this to your home address in case your son or husband opened the mail, so I thought I would mail it to your office." Well, that explained it!

13

Arthur

People fascinate me. I had plenty of opportunities to meet interesting clients when I worked at a brokerage firm.

Arthur was a retired businessman, the type that you knew had worked diligently throughout his life. He was gentle, calm, and soft-spoken, and he was one of our top clients. He and his wife once took me and another coworker to lunch.

Arthur was rather plump, had rosy cheeks, and looked healthy and robust for his age—early seventies. His massive curly white hair made him look distinguished. He was a pleasant-looking older gentleman. Once every quarter, he showed up at our office to discuss his investments. He was kind and nice to talk with, both on the phone and in person.

I learned that as a young man, Arthur had started his business out of his garage, delivering goods. Later, he became a distributor, and beyond that I have no further knowledge of what he had done, except that he was successful in what he did.

One day when he called the office to check on something, I decided to ask him a personal question.

"At this point in your life, what is most important to you?" I asked, and hastily added that my question had nothing to do with investing or his portfolio and that I wanted to learn from the wisdom he had gained in life.

Arthur was quiet for a few seconds, but then chuckled.

"I suppose one's faith and family are the two most important things in life." And he did not say anything more.

For several days I pondered Arthur's response. To him, faith and family were most important at that stage of his life. But were those two sufficient for a good and happy life? For a well-balanced life, I added two more words: fitness and financial security. To be healthy and financially secure also contributed to a good and happy life. Balancing all aspects of one's life: physical, spiritual, social, and financial, is essential in keeping the wheel of life well-rounded.

Arthur was on the right track but maybe he didn't have enough time to verbalize his complete thoughts on the subject—I suppose my question had taken him by surprise!

14

Scrooge and a Christmas Turkey

It is fun to emulate Charles Dickens. I'm no Dickens, though. But I am the lonely assistant!

S crooge peered over his lenses and said harshly, "There will be no Christmas turkey this year."

The lonely assistant mustered up her courage and faintly asked, "But why, sir?"

"Because this is a festive time of the year. People have plenty to eat, and they are all on a diet. We will do our employees a great favor by not having a turkey at the office potluck."

"Whatever you say sir!" The assistant bent her head and slowly walked out of her boss's office.

By his own admission, Scrooge had managed to eat two breakfasts that morning: one at home and the other at a nearby hotel where he attended a Rotary Club breakfast meeting, which he had forgotten but remembered just in the nick of time.

"That is final," yelled Scrooge from behind. "The office will not pay for a smoked turkey. Salads will be sufficient."

In the meantime, the office girls were scurrying around, humming and giggling, and asking, "Where is the meat?" A mild-mannered employee now and then poked his head into the lonely assistant's office and reminded her that he could easily get a smoked turkey for a meager twenty dollars. Surely the office could pay for it.

The assistant was bewildered, and her heart ached. She was torn between obeying the command from her boss, Scrooge, and the desire to have meat for the girls at the office potluck. These girls, on their meager salaries, bought food and baked goodies for the office periodically. Now all they wanted was a turkey with the salads they were providing. Oh God, how could she soften the heart of Scrooge to let the girls have a turkey?

Suddenly, she saw a ray of hope. The lonely assistant smiled broadly. There was a solution after all. If the mighty men in the office were willing to donate a dollar each, there would be enough money to purchase a turkey. An envelope was passed around the office with great hope and anticipation. Joy was in the air, and the vision of a turkey was taking shape. The girls licked their lips. Was it possible to have meat at the potluck after all? Some generous souls in the office even donated two dollars, commenting that they were sure they would eat more than two dollars' worth of turkey meat.

The following morning, the envelope which was securely locked in one of the girls' desks, was returned to the assistant. Her heart began to pound as she emptied the contents and began counting. Alas, they were three dollars short.

They had come a long way. The goal of having a smoked turkey was almost within reach. The humming girls kept licking their lips and asking, "Are we there yet?"

It was Tuesday morning, and Scrooge had just returned from a lavish office Christmas party held at the regional office in San Francisco. Surely, he would be happy to see what his assistant had done to try to secure meat for the office potluck and keep the girls happy. She proudly took the envelope to Scrooge to secure his one dollar, while secretly wishing he would throw in three dollars instead.

At the sight of the envelope, all hell broke loose. Scrooge scolded the assistant for her lack of understanding and insubordination. He accused her of not carrying out his instructions and condemned her inability to communicate properly.

"I specifically said no meat," roared Scrooge.

"But sir, you said the office would not pay for it . . ." the assistant said faintly.

Scrooge had no patience to listen to any reason or explanation. The assistant had no choice but to suggest that she would return the money to the mighty men of the office and let the girls pay for all the food and do all the cooking and baking.

"Hell, no!" snapped Scrooge. "If I let you do that, you will look really bad, and I don't want you to look bad."

"That is nice of you sir!" exclaimed the assistant. She looked up and gazed into the face of Scrooge. Whatever she saw, it made her sense of humor return.

Suddenly, she remembered the motto on a button she secretly wore during stressful situations in that office. The button said: "What the fuck!" No one knew about the button or its inscribed motto, but it had lifted her spirit and made her smile on many occasions.

The smile was forcing itself into laughter, but the assistant had to restrain herself and keep a straight face. She didn't want Scrooge to think she was mocking him.

She turned around and walked away, murmuring the motto to herself. She opened the bottom drawer of her desk where she kept her purse, picked up three dollars, stuffed the money in the envelope, and ran to Nigel, the employee who could get a smoked turkey for the office Christmas potluck for exactly twenty dollars.

The girls had their meat after all.

15

Cross Section of a Life

As a believer, I submit to the will of God. Only He knows the outcome!

Frank was a recent PhD graduate from a prestigious university when my husband offered him a job in his department. We immediately liked the young man. He was pleasant-looking, quiet, agreeable, hardworking, and well-educated.

Once Frank settled in his job and secured an apartment in town, his wife joined him. I was most eager to meet her. With his qualifications, I wondered what type of woman he was married to. Or the other way around, who had snatched him?

His wife, Debbie, was strikingly beautiful—the type that turned heads. One look and you wanted to turn around and look again. She was tall and slender with shoulder-length soft brown hair, perfect delicate features, light brown eyes, a straight nose, full lips, and silky-smooth skin. It was easy for colleagues and co-workers to take notice of him and his wife, despite his very quiet disposition.

All was well, if you only looked at Debbie and admired her from a distance, because the moment she opened her mouth, one's opinion of her would change quickly. I knew nothing of Debbie's educational background, but conversation with her was always mundane. Engaging her in conversation was always easy—she talked non-stop about nothing of substance. Because she talked incessantly, with no pause or punctuation, her words sounded like gibberish. Her nervous chatter was empty of meaningful content. Sometimes she even worked herself up into a frenzy over imaginary situations that had not happened or were very unlikely to occur. One little example is enough to give you a picture of Debbie's logic and thought process.

The young man's elderly father was planning to visit them. Debbie showed me the spare bedroom where her father-in-law was going to stay. She pointed to a newly refurbished dresser in the room.

"This is an old dresser, but we just had it refinished for the guest bedroom."

"It looks really nice," I said.

"Yes, but if his father puts his suitcase on top of it, there will be scratches."

"I don't think he will," I replied.

Oblivious to my comment, she continued: "And when I see scratches, I'm going to get angry and bound to say something nasty."

"But he won't!" I repeated, almost pleadingly.

"And when I'm angry at the old man and his actions, I will say things about him that will upset my husband."

I just looked at her in utter disbelief.

"And when we both get upset, our marriage will be rocky, and we will get into a fight."

"But, Debbie, Frank's father isn't here yet—these things have not happened." I said again.

"I think it is best if his father doesn't come for a visit," she said, and that was her conclusion.

Her logic when discussing just about any subject was twisted, and she followed her own mental reasoning for making decisions about people, situations, and events.

I sometimes wondered where and how she and Frank had met and what had prompted him to marry her. Frank, as far as I could tell, was an intelligent man with a totally different mental attitude and outlook.

Life went on for a few years. He kept working and doing a good job, and she appeared with him at different office functions and parties. Then they built a house, and I thought, "Aha, maybe they are getting ready to have a family." As usual, he was very quiet, never talked much, and perhaps that is why she talked so much, for both of them. They moved into their new house and bought a second car. But still there was no talk about having a baby.

One early afternoon, Debbie called and said she wanted to come over and talk. That day is still vivid in my mind. As she sat in the Papasan chair in my living room, she crossed her long legs, tossed her long brown hair over one shoulder, and immediately announced:

"I'm going to divorce Frank."

"What?" I said it so loudly that I almost jumped at my own raised voice. "But why?"

"He won't be faithful to me, and I want to be the first one to bail out."

Thousands of questions rushed into my head, but I only asked, "Has he been unfaithful to you? You guys just built that beautiful house and bought your second car. What is going on?"

"He travels for his job," (I knew that, so did my husband) " and on his last trip he took the office secretary out to dinner." She said with deep anger in her voice.

"How do you know that?"

"He told me himself."

"So, did anything happen?"

"No, but it will. First it is dinner, then a kiss on the cheek, and you know where it will lead to."

"No, Debbie, I don't." I said vehemently.

"Well, I'm going to file for divorce and that is that. I don't even want to have any kids by this man."

"You know this is weak reasoning for getting a divorce," I said calmly.

"There is something else."

"What?" I asked.

"We have no sex life."

At this time, the front door opened, and my sons walked in from school—Kas and Matias, our exchange student from Argentina. I didn't want to probe or keep the conversation on Debbie and Frank's private life. Luckily, both boys went upstairs to their rooms.

Debbie continued in low voice, "With our poor sex life and him taking the secretary out to dinner, the future is clear to me—we have no future together. I'm moving out. He can keep the house. We won't go through lawyers—why pay those guys when we can settle things ourselves?"

It was dusk by then, and we had not even bothered to turn the lights on. I was about to cry. I felt sad for both of them, especially Frank. It crossed my mind that for some reason, she enjoyed torturing him!

Their divorce was amicable, as far as I could tell, but he looked devastated. She moved out of the house, and he let her take anything she wanted. During this time, his elderly father died. It was such a miserable time for this young man. I thought he deserved better in life.

In less than a year, he met someone, Carmella, a very good-looking woman with a business of her own. Carmella was ready to have a husband and settle down. She had been travelling abroad, and had lived with a man overseas, but it did not end up in marriage.

Frank introduced her to us. We liked her immediately. She was worldly, sophisticated, interesting, and less talkative than his first wife. Regarding appearance, they were totally compatible. She was relaxed with him and did not make him agitated or nervous. She was a fun, bohemian artist type.

Neither of them was a teenager. They entered into the relationship with their respective life experiences. He had a nice house, so she moved in with him very quickly.

Although they were divorced, Debbie had a key to the house and soon became aware of the presence of another woman in her ex-husband's life. At some point, I heard the two women had met. Smart Carmella wanted to know why Debbie had left this seemingly perfect man.

The new girlfriend, a hard-working business-woman, recognized all the good qualities in Frank and wouldn't let go. Knowing of our long friendship with Frank and the respect he had for our opinion, Carmella called me in my office one day and said she wanted to have lunch with me.

We met at a nearby restaurant. Bluntly but pleasantly, she solicited my help in advising and encouraging Frank to marry her.

"But I can't tell him what to do. He should feel comfortable and decide on his own." I said rather surprised.

"I know we are good for each other. Actually, I know we are perfect for each other. But he is scared to have a leash around his neck."

"Then provide a longer invisible leash!" I said jokingly.

Two days later, Frank called and wanted to have lunch with me. I was becoming a marriage consultant! Although I was pleased that they both respected my opinion, I couldn't really tell either party what to do. It was a decision they had to make on their own. He had gone through seven years of marriage with someone who had left him abruptly. She had lived with a man for several years, but it did not end up in marriage.

During lunch with Frank, I realized his thoughts revolved around having a prenuptial agreement. He hastened to tell me that Carmella had agreed to sign anything he proposed to her. I pondered this.

"Let's face it, Frank. You are not a wealthy man. Granted you have a nice house, have good education, and a stable job. Is there anything else?"

"No, that is it," he said

"Okay, then, if you think she is the right woman for you, that she loves and respects you, why show mistrust by having her sign such a paper?" He thought about my question for a while, and then agreed with me.

The rest is history. They had a beautiful wedding. She even decorated her own wedding cake and arranged for a lovely reception—she was a woman of many talents. She was elated to be Mrs. Frank, and I noticed he smiled often and talked more.

When Carmella became pregnant, I threw a baby shower for her. Their beautiful little girl was born, a combined image of both parents—with her mother's look and her father's coloring.

But the story doesn't end here.

Carmella was a creative woman, and Frank had a good head for business, finance, and money. It was a perfect union. Frank invested in her business, and with his financial backing and support, she could dream big. And she did.

A couple of years into their marriage, a local newspaper featured her successful business. They accomplished things together quietly without much fanfare or showing off. Occasionally, Carmella talked about her future plans and dreams for expanding her business. To me, a bookworm and an academician, they sounded far-fetched. But Carmella had creative vision. She could picture things in her mind. With Frank's help and support and their hard work, they accomplished their goals.

If Debbie, the first wife, had not initiated the divorce, they would probably have remained married as Frank was not the type to have left her. Admittedly, my husband and I worried about the young man and Debbie's strange behavior. But in retrospect, I've learned not to put a question mark where God had put a period. Frank and Carmella's little girl is now a beautiful woman and is following in her mother's footsteps. She is destined and groomed to take the helm of the family business—she has inherited all the good characteristics from both parents.

Carmella was right. She and Frank were not just good, but perfect for each other. And I'm sure Frank is happy that he didn't press the prenuptial agreement!

16

Going Back to College

"I have taught parents, and then years later, I have taught their children. But I have never taught a mother and son at the same time!" This is what my statistics professor said to me. He was also an advisor on my doctoral dissertation.

When I decided to go back to college after twenty-five years of marriage, my son was applying to medical schools. We ended up at the same college campus the same year but in different fields of study.

He was in his first year of medical school, taking heavy-duty science and statistics classes. I was in my first year of a PhD program at the college of education. He was sharing a house with three other medical students. I had rented a furnished basement apartment near the campus, only a few blocks from his home.

We seldom saw each other. He was busy with his classes and anatomy labs, and I had a full course load in addition to handling micro-teaching labs, which was my job for the assistantship I had received.

Since I had my own classes during the day, I opted to conduct micro-teaching lab sessions either early in the morning or late in the evening, slots I knew would be hard for married graduate students to take due to their family situation. I was by myself on the campus, still married, but determined to fulfill a life-long dream of getting a doctoral degree.

From day one, I focused on adjusting to campus life, taking the right courses so that I wouldn't be wasting time, and thinking of my research and dissertation plans—quite a load for a forty-eight-year-old woman. There is something to be said for a mature graduate student! I knew exactly why I was on campus and what I wanted to accomplish. So there was no time to waste.

Most education majors put off the dreaded statistics course till the end, but I signed up for it right away. I'll never forget the first day of that class. The professor—tall, with crew-cut hair and thick, black-rimmed glasses—walked into a large lecture hall. The aisles were lined up with students, some even sat on the steps. Without much fanfare, the professor started writing formulas on the center white-board. He filled the white boards on the side as well. When he was done, he turned around to face the students and said, "Well, this is what you should remember from the course prior to this one!"

There were plenty of seats available in that hall for the next session, and only four students from the college of education still remained. I was one of them.

With laser-sharp focus on my work, I was busy from 6:00 a.m. until 9:30 p.m., when I came back to my tiny basement apartment and started on my own homework to get ready for the next day's classes. I had no time to socialize, but once in a while I would hear from my son.

He had a key to my apartment and would leave notes such as, "Mom, I came by and ate the leftover spaghetti," or "Mom, I came by to use the computer and printed some stuff." He was as busy as I was.

It was time for mid-term exams. Despite my hard work, I ended up with a D on a psychology exam. When I saw that red D, I wanted the earth to open up and swallow me. Unfortunately, there was no time to wallow in my own sorrow and sadness. I had to conduct a micro-teaching class for undergraduates and finish the day before going to my place of solitude.

As soon as I walked into my tiny apartment, I dropped my briefcase on the bed, sat at the kitchen table, and began wailing. I was crying so loudly that I did not notice someone had entered the apartment.

Suddenly, I felt my son's arms around me, hushing me.

"Mom, what is it? Are you okay?" he asked, alarmed at having found me crying. I nodded.

"Is Dad okay?" he asked. Again, I nodded.

"Then what is it?" I picked up the test and while hiccupping, pointed to the D and started wailing again, louder this time. He hugged me and kept saying, "Calm down, hush . . ."

While crying, in that very moment in the back of my mind I was thinking, *Who is the child here? Who is the parent? Woman, get a grip on yourself!*

Suffice to say, my son consoled me and advised me to go talk to the professor, and then he left. I stopped crying, washed my face, consumed half a pint of ice cream in a hurry, and then got to work preparing for the next day's classes. I reminded myself no one had forced me to go back to college. I was doing it for me.

I talked to the professor. She helped me figure out how to study for her class. I did not drop the course but worked harder. Her expertise in the field was valuable, and she recommended an instrument for testing students that I later used to conduct my doctoral research.

The statistics class was the killer, but we formed study groups and worked our hearts out. I ended up taking another course with the same professor, Dr. Everson, because I knew it would help me with the research project.

When the year ended, I wandered into the mathematics department to have a chat with Dr. E. He was not in his office, but I could hear him in another colleague's office. The door was open and I was in the hallway, so I could hear their conversation. He was obviously talking to a novice professor.

"This is how I handle the situation and weed out those who are not serious about statistics." He was chuckling.

"On the first day of class, I put a whole bunch of nonsense formulas on the board, and tell them they should know all of these from the previous class. The serious ones will show up again. The others won't." Then he laughed loudly.

Aha, that is what Dr. Everson was doing! I was glad I didn't give up. As grueling as his statistics course was, I benefited from his knowledge and expertise and was able to complete a quantitative research study.

While I was taking his class, he was also teaching medical students the intricacies of statistical reports on various drugs in the field of medicine. I have never compared notes on the subject with my son, but I sometimes wonder if Dr. E. played the same phony formula jokes on medical students as he did on us! Most likely not.

17

Meeting Phil Batt: A Memory

The strange world of politics!

At the age of forty-eight, after twenty-five years of marriage, I decided to go back to school. I had a specific plan and goal in mind. I wanted to research the role of intrinsic motivation in children's academic success. The desire to research intrinsic motivation came about as a result of my work at a brokerage firm. I had closely observed those employees who motivated themselves in order to achieve their goals. But those who waited to be enticed by an outside stimulus only reached a certain degree of success.

How could I discover the root of internal motivation in children? Could it be cultivated and translated into academic success? That was my goal.

To conduct my research, I chose two sites. One of them was the town of Wilder, a small rural community in southern Idaho. Wilder is known for its onion fields and other agricultural products. I chose this site because the place was populated by Hispanic farm workers and their families. The children of these migrant workers were the subject of my study.

For three months, every day, I drove the forty miles from my house in Boise to Wilder. Consequently, I got to know the superintendent of their schools, the teachers, students, and their families. It was part of my research design to test the kids and interview their parents. And the community got to know me, too.

But my research is not the focus of this story.

I think it was *Cinco de Mayo* celebration in Wilder. I spent the whole day in that town. I celebrated with the locals, bought stuff from the vendors—I distinctly remember buying a set of Raggedy Ann and Andy handmade dolls—listened to lovely Mexican music, and met more of the local folks. That is when I met Phil Batt for the first time.

After having walked up and down the main street, we both stopped and began a conversation. I had heard his name, but I didn't know that he was an onion farmer and had connections to Wilder. Later on, I learned he was born in Wilder.

Phil was thinking about running for governor on the Republican ticket. We talked, and he appeared to be genuinely interested in my research and the fact that I was a grad student at the University of Idaho. He then asked if he and I could meet in Boise. Phil was a short man with white hair and a friendly, grandfatherly face. He must have been in his late sixties.

A few weeks later, we met again, and he asked for my resume. He wanted to know more about my research related to Hispanic children.

He said if he won the election in November, he would like for me to have a job in his administration. He took down my information, and we parted.

Phil Batt did win the election and became the governor of Idaho in 1995. In the meantime, I had completed my research project, received my PhD, and was looking for a job, teaching college or otherwise.

My husband and I attended Phil Batt's inauguration party at the state capitol. It was a fun evening with food, music, merriment and lots of mingling with friends.

The new governor was putting his own people in place. I received a call from a chubby young man whom I had seen around Phil. I assumed he was acting as an assistant, a gofer of sorts whose role was to help Phil. He called and set up an appointment for me to attend a meeting to be interviewed. Here comes the most interesting part because I had never been interviewed for a government job.

The day of the meeting, I arrived at the capitol building and entered a large conference room. Tables and chairs were set up in a U shape. Phil was sitting at the head of the table with an empty chair next to him, where I was directed to sit. Other chairs were occupied by men, a few of whom I recognized. They were big honchos from the Republican party. I was being interviewed by the whole clan!

I don't remember the exact questions they asked—the whole experience was new to me—but I do recall that I was emphasizing my trust and allegiance to Phil Batt, who I knew was a decent guy. Maybe they did ask about my research.

A week later, I received another call from the same chubby young man to meet with him. It was in a small room, again in the capitol building. He had a book of printed computer sheets. He put it in front of me and said to leaf through the pages and see if there was a job that interested me!

Based on repeated comments by my advisor, Dr. Judy Doerann, who reminded me often to be proud of my quantitative research, I wanted to have a job where my knowledge of the migrant children and their education could be utilized.

"Phil is in Arizona now, but he has asked me to meet with you and offer you a job," the young man said.

Wow, is this how it works? The names I saw on those printed pages, the ones I recognized, were decent folks, and they were doing a good job. How could I take over their position, willy-nilly? I voiced my concern and objection.

"Because they will do the same to us when they win the election." He smirked and threw me a half-glance.

In all honesty, I could not point to any job I wanted. I was disillusioned by the process. How could I replace one of these people when they were doing such a good job?

"I have no idea which job to choose, and it is up to you to decide if you think my educational background and research could be useful somewhere." I said to the young man and left the meeting.

Naïve? Yes, I know!

Needless to say, I never heard from Phil Batt or his administration again.

A year later, I was driving north to the University of Idaho in Moscow with two very remarkable women. One was Marilyn Shuler, the human rights and civil rights activist, well-known and respected in Boise and the director of the Idaho Human Rights Commission. The other one, Donna Shepard, was the widow of deceased Allan Shepard, a supreme court justice in Idaho in the 1980s. Marilyn and I were both on the advisory board of the Martin Peace Institute at the University of Idaho, and were going up there to attend the annual meeting.

We had a fabulous time on the drive up, laughing, eating and discussing issues—a memorable hamburger lunch at a small café in Riggins, Idaho, finished off with their famous blackberry cobbler. It was during this lunch that I re-told the process of the interview and what I had said to Phil Batt's young assistant.

"You said what?" Donna asked incredulously. Both ladies stopped eating and stared at me with half open mouths. Then they burst out laughing and declared I was too honest and not cut out to be in politics!

I completely agreed with them—I never divulged that one of the jobs listed on that computer sheet that was offered to me was Marilyn's!

18

Children's Library, My Favorite

As a patron of Highlands Ranch Library in Colorado, I wrote the following piece which appeared in the Douglas Country News Press in October 2007. Some of the best writing we've got is in the children's room.

A lot of parents take their young children to the library. I did the same when my son was young. And since we moved across the country from Iowa to Illinois to Indiana and then to Idaho—exhausting all the "I" states—we had the privilege of visiting many different libraries. This may not sound like a big deal, but what I want to share is how I myself benefited by going to children's libraries.

Having a graduate degree in any particular field usually means we know a good amount about that specific field. It also means that we probably have researched and learned a great deal about one specific topic. It was only after I earned my doctorate that I realized how much more there was to know.

Having had my early schooling in another continent, I also recognized the fact that there were times when I was at a disadvantage when it came to having certain background information. It felt like hitting potholes here and there on the education highway. That is when the children's libraries came to my assistance.

Basic knowledge about any topic is always the starting point. For example, when I felt the desire and the need to learn about the history of the United States, I dashed to the children's library and gave myself a crash course in U.S. history in simple language, because the facts don't change. Or, when I became interested to learn about all the U.S. presidents and their wives, my first stop was at the children's library. I had no idea Abigail Adams argued the cause of women's rights with her husband, John Adams, in 1776, and that it was Eleanor Roosevelt who transformed the role of First Lady and made it acceptable for the First Lady to have a life of her own.

From Martha Washington to Laura Bush, and all the First Ladies in between, I gained basic information about these women and their contributions, great or small, to our nation by reading books in the children's section of the library.

To learn the simple and basic version of any topic, such as history, geography, government, economics, law, art, religion, or even foreign languages, one can start at the children's section.

We can always expand on the information and augment the basic knowledge by reading more sophisticated material from the grown-up section. For example, I let Gore Vidal expand my knowledge by taking me into the minds and private rooms of presidents Washington, Adams, and Jefferson, and I let Cokie Roberts teach me about the "Founding Mothers," the women who raised our nation.

When I see young mothers take their children to the library—particularly if, like me, they come from diverse cultural backgrounds—I think of all the basic information that is right there at their fingertips.

I'm a grandmother now and my grandchildren live in Seattle, but I have no qualms about walking into the children's library all by myself. The staff is always friendly and ready to help. I pretend I'm an elementary school teacher who is getting ready to assign research work to her students—only I'm the student.

19

From the Diary of an Educator

It is the fall semester and the first day of classes
at the college where I teach.

I am an early riser and prefer to get to school at least an hour before my first class. Arriving early has its advantages, one of which is the almost-empty parking lot. I can park anywhere I want without hassle.

It is almost 7:00 a.m. when I walk into the building of the college where I teach. Hauling my heavy briefcase, I pass by a long rectangular table along the wall in front of the computer lab. This table is usually used by vendors or college recruiters. I see the profile of a woman sitting at this table, slightly facing the wall, squeezing her elbows together and quietly talking into a cell phone. With a quick glance, I notice she is crying, but she has strategically placed her backpack on the long table and is clutching the cell phone in her right hand, to make sure no one can see her face as the tears flow from her eyes.

I pass her, pretending I have not noticed anything. But then I stop and turn around abruptly. I walk up to her and gently put my hand on her shoulder and ask, "Are you all right?"

She turns her head and looks up at me, then whispers into the phone to whomever she is talking to, "I've got to go. I will call you later."

I repeat my question, "Are you okay? What is wrong? Can I help you?"

With teary eyes, she admits it is her first day of coming back to school after many years. She feels so overwhelmed and scared that she is ready to return her books and quit.

We talk for fifteen minutes. I learn that she has come back to school to get a degree in mortuary science. She has registered for three courses: anatomy, business law, and accounting. She says she has done mortuary work for several years, and now she is planning to get a degree in that field. At that very moment, she has such cold feet that she is ready to throw in the towel, return the books and head back home.

I share with her that I experienced something similar once upon a time—going back to school after twenty-five years of marriage to get a graduate degree. I share with her my anxieties and how terrified I had felt. Just like her, I had seen young students zipping in and out of classes, and had thought I would not be able to be as agile or ready to do the academic work. But I was wrong. I share all of this with Roseanne—that was her name. I tell her as an older student, she has gained certain experiences that younger ones do not have, and that counts for a lot. I tell her she can draw on those experiences, all she needs is the confidence to believe in herself that she can do it. I encourage her to go to the cafeteria, get herself a cup of tea or coffee, wipe her tears, and walk confidently into the classroom, knowing that she has life experiences. After all, she is doing this for herself. I assure her that she knows more than what she gives herself credit for. I tell her that her feelings are normal.

Roseanne thanks me profusely, wipes her eyes, and we part.

Did my words of encouragement make any difference? I don't know, but I sure hope Roseanne did not give up her dream.

Top: Manijeh and Khosrow graduate
from the University of Tehran in 1965.

Middle: Manijeh's graduation photo,
University of Tehran.

Bottom: Manijeh receiving her Ph.D.
from the University of Idaho in 1994.

Top: Khosrow and Manijeh on
their wedding day. Her mother
made the gown.

Left: On their first wedding
anniversary.

Middle: Bruno Gegenschatz and Manijeh at Andre's Confiserie Suisse. After 49 years in Denver, Andre's closed its doors in December of 2015, and Bruno Gegenschatz officially retired.

Left: Manijeh and her mother were frequent lunch visitors at Andre's European restaurant, well-known for its tortes, pastries, quiches and other European specialties.

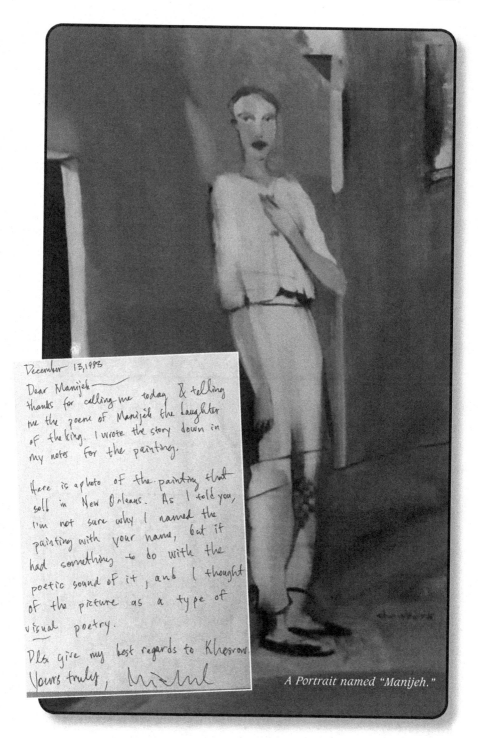

December 13, 1998

Dear Manijeh—
thanks for calling me today & telling
me the poem of Manijeh the Laughter
of the king. I wrote the story down in
my notes for the painting.

Here is a photo of the painting that
sold in New Orleans. As I told you,
I'm not sure why I named the
painting with your name, but it
had something to do with the
poetic sound of it, and I thought
of the picture as a type of
visual poetry.

Pls give my best regards to Khosrow.
Yours truly,

A Portrait named "Manijeh."

*Above: Dottie and Ray Fisher who welcomed us into their home when we
arrived in the U.S.*

*Below: My favorite photo of Dottie and Ray Fisher—boating on Red Fish
Lake, Idaho.*

Left: Dottie and Ray Fisher with Manijeh in Ames, Iowa.

Middle: The house on West Street in Ames with the attic apartment that was home during the summer of 1968.

Bottom: Dottie Fisher and Manijeh.

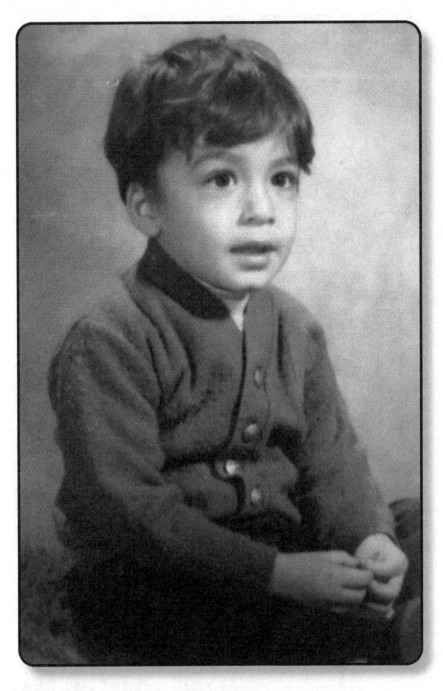

Kasra Ray, age two, in his Mr. Rogers cardigan.

Top: Khosrow, Manijeh and Kasra.

Bottom: Ronit Hanani and baby Kasra, Dryden Hall 1969. The Hanani family were our neighbors and we baby sat for each other.

Top Left: Manijeh at the age of 10.

Top Right: Manijeh the age of 23.

Bottom Left: Khosrow and Manijeh at a wedding reception in 1966.

Bottom Right: Manijeh on a trip to Venezuela in 1991.

Top: *Khosrow and Manijeh emulating sixty's style for a friend's retirement party.*

Right: *Khosrow, Manijeh, and Kasra in 2019.*

20

Bruno and Me

This is the story of a man named Bruno and his famous Swiss restaurant and pastry shop, Andre's, close to Cherry Creek Mall in Denver, Colorado.

When you were fifteen, did you know for certain what you wanted to do for the rest of your life? Amazingly Bruno Gegenschatz did! This is his story.

Bruno was only fifteen and a half when he began his training as a pastry chef in Switzerland. He admitted, always with a chuckle, that half-way through his training, he wanted to quit. His father wisely urged him to finish what he had started, then switch to something else. If it is logical to assume that we love doing what we are good at, then by the time Bruno had finished his training he was so good at it that he no longer wanted to change his profession.

Bruno was the middle child of six siblings and grew up in Wildhaus,

Switzerland, a small village of about 800 people. By the time he completed his training in Switzerland, he was an independent young man and decided to go to Australia.

"Why Australia?" I asked him once.

With a gentle smile, Bruno reminisced. "In the sixties, Australia needed young, healthy, professional immigrants and was offering a set amount of money to attract those who were willing to migrate.

So, Bruno went to Sydney in the fall of 1961.

He spent two and a half years in Sydney and married his girlfriend, Rosa, also from Switzerland. Then, in 1964, both of them came to the United States for the first time to attend the World's Fair in New York City.

"I really liked America," he confessed. He chose not to return to Australia and came directly to Kansas City instead. He worked as a pastry chef at the original Andre's, which had been in existence since 1952.

The climate in Kansas City surprised Bruno. He was actually shocked, although he refused to use the word "shock" when I talked to him. He spent over two years working at Andre's in Kansas. Then he opted to go back to Switzerland for additional training, to learn the art of sugar blowing. When he and Rosa returned to the United States, they headed directly to Denver.

"All along I had planned to come to Colorado!" he said with a chuckle.

In 1967, Bruno opened his own restaurant called Andre's in Denver. He kept the original Andre's style, whereas the one in Kansas City had been modified and was run by the third generation of its original owner. The folks back in Kansas City mentored and advised this young man and his wife who put their hearts and souls into their new restaurant.

Rosa, his wife, managed the restaurant and was the cook for nearly five years. At the time of my conversation with Bruno, she was no longer working at the restaurant, but she was still in charge of planning and altering the lunch menu, which she set every two weeks in advance.

With a twinkle in his eyes, Bruno explained that at the beginning Rosa was only managing the place and they had a German cook named Martha. Apparently, Rosa and Martha did not get along, and Rosa fired her.

"You fired her. Now you take over the cooking," Bruno told his wife. And she did for five years.

Bruno strongly believed that quality was reason for Andre's success as a restaurant. His dream was to create a unique place and offer tasty and quality food with a European flair.

That taste, quality, and European flair were my first introduction to Andre's restaurant way back in 1971.

II

In 1971, my husband was finishing up his doctoral work at Northwestern University. A professional seminar at Colorado School of Mines brought us to Denver. Lunch at Andre's restaurant was one of the activities arranged for the spouses of conference participants.

I recall having lunch with a group of ladies at a charming little restaurant that offered only two items. The decision-making process was easy, either this or that. What impressed me the most was the sight of a silver tray full of beautiful pastries offered at the end of the meal. It was the grand finale. That particular lunch and the presentation of the pastries stuck in my memory for many years.

My husband completed his research, and we moved from Illinois to Indiana and then to Idaho. Through the ups and downs of family and corporate life, lo and behold, we ended up in Denver in 1996. The memory of the little European restaurant with two items on the menu and its pastries suddenly emerged. But for the life of me, I could remember neither the name of the place nor its location.

One day, standing in line at the post office, I struck up a conversation with a couple ahead of me. It must have been lunch time because the conversation turned to food. I recounted my old story about a restaurant with delicious European pastries. The gentleman immediately interrupted me and said, "Oh, you mean Andre's."

Voila! That was the name. He gave me hasty directions on how to get there and moved on.

Armed with confidence that I had the name and the directions, I called up a friend and invited her to have lunch with me at Andre's. She lived north of Denver and said she would meet me at the restaurant.

I was a newcomer to Denver, I had no cell phone and did not consult a map! Consequently, I had a terrible time trying to find this restaurant. Not knowing where I was headed, and being late for the lunch appointment, I pulled up to the parking lot of a church.

I sheepishly asked if I could use their phone to call my friend who had been waiting for me at a restaurant. The church secretary asked for the name of the place. The mention of Andre's brought a huge smile to her face. She agreed that a newcomer would find it a bit challenging to locate the restaurant.

"But once you go there, you will never forget the way," she hastily added. By this time, the pastor had also joined in the conversation, and they both praised the food.

Since 1996, I've been a frequent visitor at Andre's for special occasions, or for no occasion at all. I invited my husband to have lunch with me—at first glance, he thought the place was "for women only!"

"Rest assured, honey, men eat here too!"

When my mother was living with me, Andre's was her favorite place to have lunch. I've also recommended the restaurant to out-of-town visitors.

III

Some people are wine connoisseurs. I'm connoisseur of pastries! I've also been a college professor hooked on assessment and evaluation. It is not surprising that in my own mind, I've always given Andre's pastries a solid A. It is also a known fact that my hobby is baking, and on top of that I love sweets. If some people are said to have a sweet tooth, I must have a mouthful of them!

On a warm summer afternoon in 2001, I made a mad dash for Andre's to purchase some pastries before it closed. The owner, Bruno Gegenschatz, was outside watering the red geraniums in front of the restaurant. The lunch crowd had dispersed, and no customers were in sight. I thought it was a perfect occasion to strike up a conversation with the owner and let him know how much I've enjoyed eating lunch at his restaurant.

Smiling broadly, I also added, "Oh, I wish to visit your kitchen when all those beautiful and mouth-watering pastries are produced."

To my great surprise, with his usual calm disposition, he stated that I was welcome to visit his kitchen any time. I looked at him in utter disbelief with my eyes wide open and mouth agape. He let out a short laugh.

"Really? Are you serious? Can I come and spend a day in your kitchen— *Andre's* kitchen?" Somehow, memories of a childhood desire crept out of my subconscious: ah, to be locked up in a pastry shop with no adult supervision.

"Why not?" He asked. Then he handed me his business card: Bruno Gegenschatz. Up to that point I had always referred to him as "Mr. Andre'."

"When is a good time to visit?" thinking he was going to take back his offer.

"Any time, just make sure you let us know you are coming, and show up at four o'clock in the morning—that is when we start baking for the day."

Ouch . . .

I'm not a procrastinator, and I don't like to waste time. I asked Bruno if I could visit him the next day. It was a Friday.

"By all means" was his simple reply.

IV

Gleefully, I announced to my husband that I was going to fulfill a dream, satisfy a deep burning desire, and cross out an item on my bucket list! He was all ears.

"I'm going to visit Andre's kitchen, and I'm planning to leave the house before 4:00 a.m. tomorrow."

Whatever went through my husband's mind, he did not share with me. But the look in his eyes, the arch of his eyebrows, and the shake of his head were the physical manifestation of words such as "nuts," "crazy," and "lunatic."

Quiet streets, sleepy city, sparse traffic, and, frankly, a tinge of trepidation all contributed to my unique experience of driving to Denver at four o'clock in the morning. On that memorable Friday, before dawn, I walked through the back door into Andre's kitchen.

The sight of the kitchen with all the stainless steel appliances and equipment, the long rectangular tables, and baking pans in variety of shapes and sizes—I wasn't dreaming. I was actually in Andre's kitchen. It was such magnificent sight! For sure, I was that kid in the candy store everyone talks about. Puff pastries, breads, rolls, cakes, tarts—I was in heaven!

The folks in the kitchen were seriously at work performing their tasks at the designated stations. And I moved from one station to the next. Hazelnut coffee cakes, apricot tarts, long sheets of puff pastry ready to be made into *mille-feuille*, which I know as napoleon. My eyes were feasting, and my brain was racing to take it all in. Not much talking was going on, and each person was only concentrating on what he or she was doing.

I put on an apron and announced that I was not just spectator; they could actually put me to work. And work, I did!

V

By nine o'clock in the morning, all the baking for the day was completed. Then the cook responsible for preparing the lunch arrived. Bruno himself arrived at about the same time. On that particular day he was decorating a birthday cake, special order.

I had observed, worked, learned, answered a few phone calls from customers, and was completely satisfied with my experience. Little did I know what was about to happen.

It was 9:30 a.m. when I called my husband—from Andre's kitchen—letting him know I was about to leave and head home. I briefly shared with him that I had enjoyed the experience and had gained insight into the workings of a pastry chef.

But then there was an unexpected turn of events.

There was a sudden commotion in the area where the cook was preparing lunch. A few rapid phone calls and then I saw the assistant cook leave in a hurry. He needed to attend a serious family emergency. I lingered and asked if there was anything I could do to help. Bruno suggested I check with the cook.

The cook put me in charge of the whipped cream machine, not a difficult task.

The lunch customers began to show up. The waitresses were buzzing around, and all I had to do was press the button on the machine and put a dollop of whipped cream on the dessert plates, next to the pastries.

After a while, I looked at the other side of the kitchen and noticed the dirty dishes were coming in at a fast pace. Bruno himself was handling the task of loading the commercial dishwasher. As I learned later, the man in charge of washing dishes had not showed up that day.

It was only logical that I offer to make a significant contribution and perform serious work besides pressing the button on the whipped cream machine, so I offered to help Bruno with brushing the plates and loading the dishwasher and then stacking up the clean dishes. He was grateful and accepted my offer. For the next two hours we worked nonstop in tandem on an assembly line of dirty dishes. We handled bins of dishes, loading, unloading, and stacking up plates without a break or a word between us.

It was almost two o'clock in the afternoon when the pace slowed down. It was time for me to leave. As I was taking off my apron, Bruno invited me to have lunch with him. He said I had earned my food! This was an offer I could not refuse. I was hungry and tired. I had been up since 3:30 a.m. and had not eaten anything.

Bruno and I had a delightful lunch and conversation together. I learned about him, and he learned about me. We both had left our respective countries about the same time, the early 1960s. He appreciated my help in the kitchen. With his usual soft chuckle, he said I was the first visitor who actually worked in his kitchen.

"Others have been mere observers," he said.

I bought a loaf of French bread for my husband and headed home. It was late afternoon.

As I entered the house, I was greeted by a frazzled, weary, irate man who thought I had left Andre's in the morning. He was getting ready to call the Denver police department and ask for help locating his missing wife.

I had completely forgotten to call again to let him know I was a dishwasher at Andre's restaurant for the day.

21

Real Argo

Did you see the movie Argo starring Ben Affleck?
It was released in 2012.

October 15, 2015

As always, I wake up to my alarm playing National Public Radio. With my eyes still closed, I lie in bed and listen to the news of the day: "Kennett Taylor, the Canadian diplomat passed away at the age of 81. He was the Canadian ambassador in Iran during the 1979 hostage crisis."

The mention of Iran makes me open my eyes and sharpens my ears. I listen carefully to what follows: "He harbored six American citizens in his home after the seizure of the American embassy in Tehran on November 4, 1979."

Now I sit upright and listen to the rest of the news: "The story of the Americans and their hiding in Tehran and their eventual escape was captured in the 2012 movie *Argo*." But it makes me skeptical when I hear, "Mr. Taylor had dismissed the movie as fictional." *Oh, really?*

October 21, 2012

I visit my sister in Florida. We have a grand time together, getting bargain chocolates from Russell Stover's candy store. Needless to say, we sample some as we walk through the aisles!

After dinner, we go see the movie *Argo* with Ben Affleck playing the lead role. I'm particularly curious to see if I recognize any part of Tehran shown in the movie—if indeed it was filmed in Tehran. I'm not sure, just assuming it was.

When the movie ends, we walk out to the lobby. There is a knot in my stomach and I'm shaking all over. My sister puts her arms around me, as I'm about to cry.

"It reminded you of the incident, didn't it?" she asks gently.

The film touches me at the core, and unwillingly, I'm taken back in time, remembering an unpleasant incident that happened to me and my husband at the Mehrabad Airport in Tehran in May of 1993.

May 1993

The 1979 Islamic Revolution and the regime change followed by the Iran-Iraq war prevented me from travelling to Iran for almost twenty years. The last time I saw my parents was in 1974.

Now it is May of 1993. I'm done with the course work and data collection for my doctoral research. I feel the need for a break and the urgency to see my aging parents. Mother tells me Dad is sick.

Fifteen years have passed since the Islamic Revolution.

I gingerly approach the Interest Section of the Islamic Republic at the

Pakistani embassy in Washington D.C. I want to inquire about the necessary travel documents to visit Iran and also make sure it is okay for me to go since I'm a U.S. citizen. I'm assured there is no problem whatsoever.

Khosrow and I arrive in Tehran without incident. But when Lufthansa lands in Tehran, my heart is about to leap out of my chest. I'm excited, nervous, and scared all at the same time.

Seeing my parents after all these years reminds me of the passage of time. We are all getting older. But the major changes are what I observe in the streets of Tehran. Women are now required to cover their heads; men do not wear ties or shake hands with women, and most of them have facial hair. I see a lot more bearded men and clergy in the streets. The eight-year war with Iraq and the estimated one million casualties have left the population in a somber and melancholy mood. It is clearly noticeable; no one smiles. My father advises me to wipe the smile off my face when I'm out in the street.

My two-week trip to Tehran with all of its ups and downs, dealing with my father's sickness and family issues, adjusting to a new social order, and remembering to cover my hair when I step outside the house, plus a myriad of unpleasant experiences are nothing compared to what I go through at the Mehrabad Airport when I want to leave the country to return to the U.S. My sister and her family live in Germany, and I'm going to stop in Frankfurt and spend a couple of weeks with her while my husband continues on to the United States.

Lufthansa usually departs from Tehran around 2:30 a.m. My husband and I arrive at the Mehrabad Airport at 10:30 p.m. just to be on the safe side, because we don't know what to expect. Rules have changed, and we must pass through several check points before boarding the plane.

At our first stop we must show our Iranian passport and travel documents to a short young man sitting in a kiosk at the airport. He has pale complexion and extremely dark lips, and he is wearing a khaki uniform. As I get close to the opening of the kiosk it reeks of cigarette smoke. He looks at our passports casually, and with half-shut eyes he looks up at us without saying a word and gives us back our passports. *Thank God, he did not fuss about our U.S. citizenship, as it is indicated in our passports.*

I'm a little less nervous. We take the escalator up to the second floor, order two cups of tea, and sit and wait until it is time to go through the security.

Two lines are formed: one for men and one for women. Here I stand separated from my husband, but I can see him—his line is moving faster. All of a sudden, I notice the officer, the same tiny uniform-clad young man in the kiosk, is checking my husband's briefcase, holding his American passport, and waiving him to go through. *Oh, my God. His U.S. passport is confiscated.* I can hear my husband making objections.

"But I cannot enter the U.S. without my American passport!"

"That is your problem, not mine." The officer says with a smirk on his face.

Oh, Lord! It is my turn now. My line has moved forward and after bodily inspection by female guards, I reach the same officer who is supposed to waive me through. But he stops me and asks for my

American passport. I lie!

"I don't have my U.S. passport with me. It is in Germany with my sister. But I can give you a copy."

"Well, then, step aside, you cannot leave."

After two weeks of dealing with my father's illness, and the unpleasant and depressing social changes, right then and there I totally lose it. I scream and wail at the top of my lungs, as if I'm having a breakdown, or someone is cutting through my body! I don't care who sees or hears me. I'm not ashamed of getting hysterical.

While the officer is waiving other passengers through, he tries to push me aside, as I'm standing right next to him.

"Go and cry over there," he says frowning and waiving his hand.

"No, I won't. I'm staying right here." I'm belligerent and give a loud cry and shrill near his ears.

By this time, my husband has been sent to see the "big boss." He is trying to reason with them, pointing out that we checked with the folks in the Interest Section in Washington D.C. and had been assured there wouldn't be any problem getting in and out of the country. However, I'm totally irrational and reacting emotionally—my wailing continues. All the passengers, foreign and domestic, are wondering what is going on as they go through the big double door to board the bus to get to the plane.

Lufthansa officials are about to close the door. Although they cannot interfere and won't deal with the airport security guards, they look at me and keep asking, "Are you coming or not?"

Finally, the puny officer with dark lips says disgustingly, "Okay, you can go."

"Not without my husband!" I scream, now hiccupping because of the intensity of my wailing.

Right then, my husband returns after visiting the big boss. He shows up accompanied by another security officer. The two officers exchange glances. To save face for the first officer who has decided, willy-nilly on his own, to prevent us from leaving, the new officer gently says, "The colonel has approved for them to leave." Then he hastily adds, "Of course, it is your decision to let them go!"

The officer with the dark lips gets the drift. He gives back my husband's American passport and since he has already permitted me to leave, we are free to go. The two Lufthansa officials practically shove us through the big double door—just like the way it was in Affleck's movie— we are the last ones to board the bus.

By the time I get into the plane, I'm drenched in sweat from head to toe under the scarf and the body cover. I sit in my seat, take off the scarf, and look up and pray, "I hope this baby takes off!"

So, when I hear some say Mr. Affleck's movie was purely fictional, I ask, "Really?"

Author's note: This episode happened in 1993. The Iranian government has made changes and improvements to make it easy for Iranians who are U.S. citizens to travel back and forth to visit relatives. My subsequent visits to see my parents were smooth and without incident. It is my belief that the young, inexperienced officer acted on his own without respect for the law in order to exercise his newly-granted authority.

22

Amber

I'm a retired educator, but now and then I think about some of my former students.

Her name was Amber, and I often wonder where she is, and whatever happened to her.

Amber was one of my students during a fall semester at the college where I taught writing and composition. The very first day I entered the classroom and quickly scanned the students, I noticed her immediately. She was slender, with short blonde hair and was dressed provocatively. She had a sour and belligerent look on her face. Her posture presented total defiance and combativeness. I was puzzled, but ignored it and went on with handing out the assignment. It was a required writing assessment which normally took most of the class period. Two minutes later, Amber got up abruptly and walked out of the classroom.

Her odd behavior made me follow her out into the hallway. I pretended I was going to get a drink of water while the other students were busy writing. I reached Amber around the water fountain. She looked insanely angry and agitated, ready to explode. Pretending I was filling up my little water bottle, I asked gently and softly if she was okay.

As if she was only waiting to hear a kind word, tears gushed out of her eyes like the fountain I was pressing, and she replied vehemently, "I don't want to be in this class."

"Then why are you here?" I asked her gently.

"They made me do it; I have to." She said sobbing. "All I want is my little girl, my daughter. They have taken her away from me."

"Who forced you to take this class?" I asked, really surprised, and curious.

Through our short and quick chat near the water fountain, I learned that Amber had a little daughter born out of wedlock. Her parents forced her to enroll in college so that she could do something with her life. And if she did not stay in college, the baby was going to be taken away from her.

I gently put my hand on her shoulder.

"But you are here now, and the course is paid for. Why don't you come back to class and try to do your best," I said softly.

She slowly stopped crying, and her anger subsided a bit. Now that she had told someone about her predicament, she felt better. She did not put up a fuss, and we both walked back to the classroom together.

Amber was not a dumb blonde girl. Her responses to some class questions were coarse but to the point. Her attitude, and the way she dressed, made some of the young men in the class roll their eyes and refer to her as "hard core." Whenever she made comments, I noticed some men snickering. I tried to understand her real point of view on issues, though she had difficulty articulating them properly.

For their first writing assignment—a descriptive essay—my students were to choose their own topic and describe a person, a place, or an event. They were to paint a picture with words and create emotional feelings in the reader. Amber did this beautifully. When I was done reading her essay, which was about her aunt, I despised and hated that woman as much as Amber did.

Amber had made a mistake when she was sixteen. A one-time sexual encounter had landed her pregnant. The aunt—her father's sister—had never let her forget it. By verbal abuse, derogatory comments, unkind words, and jabbing remarks, she had robbed Amber of all her self-confidence. "Why not be what they say I am?" she must have thought to herself. Her behavior, language, and provocative clothes sanctioned whatever the aunt had said and thought of her.

Through our class discussions, I somehow conveyed to the male students and Amber herself that she was not an airhead blonde, that she had some good viewpoints on issues, and that she could contribute to serious discussions. Amber stayed and finished the semester and earned a passing grade. I never saw her again.

Where is Amber now, I sometimes wonder! Did she attend another school? Is she taking care of her little girl? I sure hope so.

23

Diary of a Mug

A beautiful mug's point of view.

I'm a nice-looking mug in a big department store. My original price tag indicates I'm worth fifteen dollars, but now I'm on sale for only five dollars. I don't feel alone because there is another mug just like me on this table for the same price! It is as if we are twins.

A woman walks to the sale table and eagerly picks me up. Then she turns me upside down. I suppose she wants to know where I was made. Definitely not in China! I'm good-looking, very colorful with an Aztec design. The blues, yellows, and reds combined with my unique twisted rope-like handle make me very attractive. I'm worth more than five dollars for sure.

The woman recognizes my worth and immediately picks up my twin as well. Both of us are wrapped in paper and put into a plastic bag. She takes us home. What does she plan to do with us? Is she going to use us for tea? Coffee? I wonder!

But the woman does not keep us in her kitchen. She goes directly down to her basement. She mutters to herself, 'These will make great gifts, and I'm going to put them on my Nancy Reagan shelf." What is a Nancy Reagan shelf?

Sure enough, there is a shelf with an assortment of items on display: candles, perfumed soaps, mugs—but not like me—picture frames, and small decorative boxes. Is this what she calls her Nancy Reagan shelf? I don't even know who Nancy Reagan is.

My twin mug and I have nothing to do but sit on the shelf waiting for something to happen. Occasionally, when the woman comes down to the basement, she inspects the shelf and just looks at the items. But she picks me up frequently and admires my colors.

After two months of sitting on the shelf doing nothing, suddenly, one day the woman walks down to the basement with a friend. There must be something going on upstairs in her kitchen. She and her friend walk toward the shelf.

"Don't worry, pick what you want from my Nancy Reagan shelf," the woman says to her friend.

"Thanks a million. I feel bad that I didn't get her a gift," the friend replies.

"Oh, for heaven's sake, don't feel bad. Pick whatever you want."

Her friend examines a few items on the shelf and then she picks me up and says, "This is beautiful. I'll take this one." The woman then provides a gift bag and some tissue paper. I'm wrapped again and put into a gift bag and taken upstairs.

Wow, there is a party going on in the kitchen. It is a retirement party for a friend and many people walk in with cards, gifts, and flowers. They give me to the person who is retiring. She looks at me approvingly and then puts me back in the bag.

I'm now in another person's kitchen. But my new owner is not interested in me at all. She is busy getting rid of all her stuff, including mugs, plates, and baskets. Actually, she is getting ready to have a huge garage sale within a week. From the conversations I overhear, I learn she has actually sold her house and is about to move away. I guess that is what retired people do. Maybe I wasn't a good gift for her after all.

The day of the garage sale, I'm put on a table along with other coffee mugs and glasses. They put a tag on me that says "ten cents." I cannot believe the degradation! I was worth fifteen dollars a few months ago at a prestigious department store. But now I'm only ten cents and haven't been used at all. I'm a brand new mug for God's sake!

It is a busy day, and many people stop by to purchase different items at the garage sale. Few people approach the table where I am placed. Suddenly, I see the woman who had first purchased me for five dollars standing near the table looking at me. The peculiar look on her face indicates her disbelief that I am priced at ten cents. There is something strange in the way she looks at me. She casually and slowly walks toward me. I can sense her determination—she wants to buy me back. But before she can extend her arm to grab me, another woman picks me up and says, "Oh, this is such a pretty mug, and only ten cents!"

I'm now going to a new house with another woman starting a new adventure. Maybe she will drink out of me. But I wonder if my twin is still a virgin, sitting on the Nancy Reagan shelf!

24

The Day I Disappeared

Sometimes, our minds can play tricks on us and cause problems!
This happened to me.

It was a miracle that no one called the campus police. I could visualize the headlines: "Adjunct Faculty Vanishes on Campus" or "Midday Disappearance of English Professor" or simply, "Where in the World is Dr. B?"

It was a bitterly cold day in December, and almost the end of the first semester. I walked into my office early in the morning, hauling my briefcase. My colleague and officemate, Don, was sitting at his desk reading the daily newspaper.

"Good morning, Don. Today is Wednesday!" I announced cheerfully.

"If you say so," Don said casually without lifting his eyes from the paper.

I settled at my desk and proceeded to open my briefcase when another colleague, Lindsay, poked her head in.

"Have you seen the security guard?" There was anxiety in her voice.

"We have not" Don and I answered in unison.

"I forgot my office keys," Lindsay explained, "and I've called the security guard to come and unlock the door, but I have given him the wrong office number!"

I tried to put her at ease.

"We all have myriads of tasks to perform, and millions of numbers to remember—passwords, deadlines, meeting times," I said. "It is not a big deal that you forgot your own office number."

I hoped my words calmed her anxiety.

I met my 8:30 class and collected their essays and writing portfolios for the semester. Then my students completed a grammar quiz. Pardon me, I never use the words quiz or test. I give my students MRI, (Mental Registration Index)—a rose is a rose by any other name!

The assigned work for the semester was complete. A few students had missed the required writing assessment due to bad weather and heavy snow; I referred them to the testing center. The class was basically over.

I decided to check out the bookstore.

On that memorable Wednesday, the bookstore was having a lavish reception along with a 20 percent discount on books and gift items for the faculty. It was a perfect opportunity to buy Christmas gifts for my grandchildren. And that is when it all happened!

Without prior warning, my brain switched on, switched off, gyrated, and somehow convinced me that it was Thursday! Based on my schedule for

Thursday, I would have an hour between my two morning classes. The fact that my students for the next class were waiting for me on the fourth floor completely escaped my mind. It was as if an invisible eraser entered my brain and skillfully wiped out any trace of the word *Wednesday*!

I leisurely walked into the bookstore, exchanged pleasantries with the staff who graciously directed me to the food section: appetizing little sandwiches, deviled eggs—and I love deviled eggs—bite-size chicken *cordon bleu*, an assortment of cookies, lemonade, and fruit punch. What a wonderful way to show appreciation to the faculty and staff. It truly was impressive.

While enjoying the food, I chose a few books and gifts for my grandchildren. I picked up a tiny stuffed bear, wearing a purple T-shirt—the color of our college. The words on the T-shirt said, "Somebody from Arapahoe Community College loves me." Ah, a perfect gift for my three-year-old granddaughter. I continued looking for more gifts at bargain prices.

In came our college president, Dr. Glandon. He quickly headed towards the sweat pants, size extra large! *Here is a man with a mission. He knows exactly what he wants!* We exchanged greetings.

I turned around and there was Jill from the human resource office. Our conversation turned to the holidays, house guests, and cooking. She confided in me that she was going to have company over the holidays, but that she was not fond of cooking and spending long hours in the kitchen. I recommended a cookbook by Rachael Ray, who is a regular on the Food Channel and normally prepares a full-course meal within thirty minutes.

"I assure you, Jill, I've tried her recipes and it truly takes only thirty minutes to put a meal together, provided you have all the ingredients on hand."

Jill was excited and said she would look for the cookbook.

I picked up another deviled egg and washed it down with a cup of fruit punch. Then Cindy walked in. Cindy and I, on many occasions, have discussed our aging parents. It was a good time to catch up with news about her parents. We engaged in a humorous conversation about the perils of old age!

I glanced toward the entrance of the bookstore and saw Marcia, a colleague from the psychology department. She was standing right in the middle of the entrance to the bookstore. Her inquisitive eyes were scanning the scene, like a camera taking a panoramic picture. As soon as I came into her view, she looked as if she had seen a ghost. She let out a short cry followed by a sigh of relief.

With a big grin on my face, I approached her.

"What's up, Marcia?"

"But . . . but you are okay?" she mumbled.

"Well, of course! Why?" I continued smiling.

"Your students are waiting for you upstairs," she said very quickly in a somewhat hushed voice.

Calm and assured, I looked at my watch, it was only 10:45, and my next class was scheduled to meet at 11:30. I had plenty of time. My relaxed demeanor annoyed Marcia.

"But the entire department is looking for you," she said emphatically, and hastily added that my department chair, Karin, was checking all the bathrooms, in case I had fainted somewhere. My students had also checked with the department secretary, Anita, to find out what had befallen their instructor. Surely, something disastrous must have happened for Dr. B not to show up in class. Colleagues who were not in the classroom at that time were mobilized to check different floors and bathrooms. Marcia had volunteered to check the first floor, hence her presence at the bookstore.

Marcia's emphatic words, laced with a tinge of anger, made me stop and think for a second.

"Today isn't Thursday, is it?" I asked meekly.

Oh, my God, how could I have been so foolish? It was Wednesday indeed. I was embarrassed beyond belief, yet I found the situation hilariously amusing. It was a peculiar combination of guilt and glee.

With the speed of light, I collected my purchases and dashed up to the fourth floor. I was bewildered by my own action and the trick my brain had played on me. Yet, I could not stop laughing.

Karin was genuinely relieved to see me. She had visions of me flat on my face on a bathroom floor. Since she could not find me, she had called my house and left a message of inquiry.

As soon as I heard the words: message, home, answering machine, I was alarmed.

"Oh, my God. Now my husband will get involved," I thought.

Khosrow knew I had left the house very early that morning. I called his cell phone. He answered.

"Hi, honey! It's me. I'm at school. I called your office, but you did not answer. Where are you?"

His brisk and serious voice replied, "I'm at your college, just about to get into the elevator, coming up to the fourth floor!"

Oh, Lord! My foolishness had caused him to leave his work and come to search for me. I couldn't face him alone. I rushed to Karin's office and begged her to accompany me to the elevator to greet my husband. I needed her support.

When my husband stepped out of the elevator, Karin and I greeted him with a big smile and we both gave him a hug.

"Yes, I heard the message and dashed out," he said.

He had followed the route I normally take to drive to college, with visions that I might have had an accident or gone off the road, and taken to the hospital, or maybe he thought I was dead. Did I see a tear in his eyes? No, it could've been the result of the very cold air outside!

The combination of embarrassment and humor lingered. I was alive and safe. But I needed to analyze my own behavior and figure out the subconscious motivation that had prompted my action. What was it? Shopping and discounted merchandise? Deviled eggs and cookies? Whatever it was, it made me go back to the bookstore for more browsing. I was glad and thankful that no one thought of notifying the campus police.

The genuine display of concern and caring by my boss, colleagues, and students made me realize how fortunate I was. They all cared about me and looked after my safety and well-being.

It was only logical that I should keep the little stuffed bear for myself, because I was convinced beyond a doubt that "Somebody from Arapahoe Community College loves me"!

25

My Right Eye

I looked at myself in the mirror. Had I been in a boxing match with Mike Tyson? Did he punch me directly in the right eye?

I had gone through a procedure called a dacryocystorhinostomy. After months of thinking, I had finally decided to go ahead and have the procedure done on my right eye.

In the process of informing my students of the upcoming surgery, and the possibility of missing one or two class sessions, I had broken the word into parts: "dacryo," "cysto," "rhinostomy." This also helped me educate myself on the procedure. Simply put it, it was the repair of a tear duct in my right eye. It was to be performed in an outpatient clinic, and I was to be driven home from the clinic by a responsible adult the same day after the surgery.

That responsible adult was my husband, who drove me to the Keiser Clinic located in Denver. We arrived at the ambulatory surgery clinic at 6:30 a.m.

Ellen, one of the many friendly nurses, greeted me with a smile. Together we walked to a partitioned room to get ready. She advised my husband to stay in the waiting area.

"Please, take off your clothes and put this on," she said as she handed me a hospital gown.

"And please, you take these homemade cookies and share them with others." I handed her a big round tin can full of cookies. They were not your regular chocolate chip cookies. I had used powdered oatmeal, shaved dark chocolate, and plenty of chocolate chips and walnuts.

The conversation turned to pastries and cakes. What a sweet way to start the day—the truth was I had been fasting for over twelve hours in preparation for the surgery.

While we talked, Ellen took my vitals, filled out a form, and then inserted a needle in my hand and hooked it to an IV. She also handed me a tiny cup containing an ounce of liquid.

"It is important to take this medicine. It neutralizes the acidity in the patient's stomach. This is for those patients who are going under complete anesthesia," Ellen explained. "Patients normally dislike this drink. Go ahead and drink it in one gulp, then it won't taste as bad."

I cheerfully complied. Salute, bottoms up, and in one gulp I emptied the cup.

At that very moment my thoughts gravitated toward my college students. As a writing professor, I was trying to figure out in my mind how to describe this totally unfamiliar drink so that they could vicariously taste what I had just swallowed.

I summoned the experiences of my taste buds and determined the drink was a combination of juices from very sour grapes and unripe cranberries. The color also resembled the combination of the two, a dull greenish light brown!

I shared my thoughts with Ellen.

"No one has ever described the taste before!" she smiled. "Patients usually just say it is 'yucky.'"

Then Ellen left the room to go get the anesthesiologist and asked my husband to come in and keep me company.

A few minutes later, a young male anesthesiologist bounced into the room. He was energetic, vivacious, and immediately embarked on pronouncing my full name and inquiring about its origin. He seemed to be only a few years older than my son, but he was definitely more talkative and outgoing. I wondered how much of it had to do with his training to put the patients at ease right before surgery, and how much was part of his own personality.

My thoughts were interrupted by the surgeon, Dr. Gardner, who poked his head in, and with a friendly smile, inquired if we were ready.

The anesthesiologist, who by this time was deep into discussing world politics with my husband, gave a nod and cheerfully declared that he had solved all of the world's problems in just a few minutes!

I got up from the chair, picked up my IV bag, made absolutely sure the designer hospital gown I was wearing was securely tied in the back, and calmly walked toward the operating room.

The exuberant anesthesiologist was standing at the head of the long and narrow operating table. He instructed me to put my head on a round, doughnut-shaped pillow.

"This looks more like a whoopee cushion to me," I quipped.

"In a second you are going to think I'm the best-looking fellow in this room."

I heard his voice from a distance, and before my mind could think of a response, I plunged into the world of unconsciousness.

26

Visiting Mister Rogers

On a small black-and-white television set in our tiny apartment in Evanston, Illinois, I saw Fred Rogers for the first time. The year was 1969, and my son was almost a year old.

I turned on the television and there was this gentle and pleasant man who looked directly at the camera and talked ever so slowly. My son was mesmerized. I had not seen *"Mister Rogers' Neighborhood"* and didn't know who he was. I momentarily thought maybe he had a speech problem!

That afternoon I mentioned it to my neighbor, Hannah Hanani, who had a five-year-old daughter. With a bit of a chuckle, I asked, "Is this guy okay?"

My neighbor laughed and said, "You are talking about Fred Rogers. Oh, it is a wonderful show for children." And she went on to say that it was a program she and her daughter watched together.

Now that I had learned something about *Mister Rogers' Neighborhood*, I was most anxious to watch it again. The rest is history. My son and I visited his neighborhood every day! I also realized that his deliberate communication style with carefully chosen words was meant for his young audience.

Fred Rogers made us feel we were special just the way we were. It was a quiet time for my son and I to listen and pay attention to what he said. We were assured we were unique and that there wasn't another person on the whole plant like us. And it was okay to be different. Watching the program with my toddler, I realized how beautiful it was to love and accept people just the way they were.

Fred Rogers also reminded us that perfect human beings have imperfections and we cannot all be the same in our appearance and ability. I agreed with him wholeheartedly. He said our uniqueness was a gift and gave us opportunities to fulfill our dreams.

Fred Rogers taught us it was okay to be angry, sad, or disappointed. At the same time, he taught us how to express our emotions in words and how to deal with these feelings. He also told us that many people felt the same way, and he reassured us that we were loved, even when we had those feelings. I chuckled when he said, "The people we love the most can make us feel the gladdest and the maddest!" How true it was.

Our daily visits with Fred Rogers caused my toddler son to want a cardigan sweater just like Mr. Rogers'. We checked every store in a nearby mall. Finally, at a JCPenney store, we found a small blue cardigan sweater with brass buttons in front. From then on, the minute the music came on and Mr. Rogers walked through the door and grabbed his sweater from the closet, my son would do the same thing. It was a ritual he did not miss.

Watching the show as an adult taught me a lot about myself and the world around me. I understood my own feelings about relationships, parenting, teaching, and learning. Those daily visits with Fred Rogers fifty years ago contributed a lot to the way I taught and conducted my classes. I perceived my students as unique individuals. My adult students brought into the classroom not only themselves but also their feelings and their experiences. And like Fred Rogers, I tried to make them realize that they were special and that I liked them just the way they were.

27

Experience at the Zoo

No act of kindness is ever lost.

We are vacationing in Arizona and taking our grandchildren to the Phoenix Zoo. We approach the gate to purchase our admission tickets.

"I have a membership pass to the Seattle Zoo. I wonder if they would honor that at the Phoenix Zoo?" my daughter-in-law, Kate, announces rather loudly.

"Or maybe at least it will be good for some discount!" I comment.

While walking and discussing the admission fee, a gentleman and his young daughter approach us.

"I have a membership pass to the Phoenix Zoo, and I have guest passes that are about to expire. I would like for you to use them," he says and offers us four free guest passes.

What an incredible act of kindness from a total stranger! Whether he heard our conversation or saw our out-of-state license plate, his generosity touches my heart. We accept his gracious offer. He introduces us as his guests and hands the extra passes to the attendant at the gate.

We thank him and then head for a different part of the zoo and don't see him again. He has saved us over fifty dollars in admission fees. I think about this experience for several days—doing something nice for total strangers when they least expect it.

This incident takes me back to my childhood and a phrase I often heard my parents say. Roughly translated from Farsi to English, it goes something like this: "Give an act of kindness at the Euphrates River; God will give it back to you in the Sahara Desert." As a child this did not make sense to me and sounded absurd.

A child's mind can't understand metaphors or grasp the deep meaning of folk wisdom. What they were trying to teach me was that an act of kindness never gets lost in this world. It only spreads and will come back to you at a time and a place where you least expect it.

As we walk around the zoo, I ponder the old proverb and try to figure out what act of kindness I performed in the past toward a stranger that is now coming back to me at the Phoenix Zoo!

Voila! I remember it.

Several years ago, my husband and I were going to a movie. I had purchased four tickets. Before entering the theater, I saw a young couple—probably on a date—getting ready to buy their tickets. Immediately, I offered them my extra two tickets. The surprised look on their faces combined with gratitude and plenty of smiles gave me a sense of incredible joy.

I'd also witnessed a random act of kindness at Denver International Airport. It was right after the September 11 tragedy, and we were flying to New York City to attend a wedding. Many people were nervous about flying at that time.

While having lunch in a small café at the airport, I saw a young man get up. He paid for his bill and the lunch of an elderly couple sitting a few tables away. It still warms my heart to remember the look on the old couple's faces and their reaction to this act of kindness from a stranger.

When they thanked the young man, he simply and cheerfully said, "Please pass it on."

Whether it is in the Euphrates of Asia or at the Phoenix Zoo or in the mountains of Colorado, no random act of kindness ever gets lost.

28

My Anniversary

"Really? You have been married fifty-five years?" a friend asks me.
"How did you do it?"

My cousin and his wife who live on the East Coast call to congratulate us. His wife asks the same exact question, and adds, "What is the secret?"

"Ever heard of the word *compromise*?" I ask her.

She giggles and says, "Yes?"

"Well, let me tell you, this is a word in the English language that needs to be written in gold, kept in sight at all times, slowly chewed, swallowed, and its meaning totally digested. Above all, it needs to be practiced."

She is quiet and gives me a chance to get on my soap box. I continue.

"When I first got married, I thought everything would be fifty-fifty. But life doesn't work that way. Sometimes it is seventy-thirty or forty-sixty. Heck, I've even experienced ninety-nine and one. But the key is to know when to compromise and make it a win-win situation—at any combination."

At this point, I suddenly remember something my mother once told me. She and my father were married almost sixty years before he passed away—and God knows he was not an easy man to live with. She once told me, "Your dad is a good man. Sometimes he can make himself as thin as a thread that can go through the eye of a needle. Other times, the big gate of a city is not wide enough for him to pass through!" I laughed, but now I think when he passed himself through the eye of the needle is probably when Mother was at 99 percent and he was at only 1 percent!

Another gem of an advice I received from my mother had to do with fabric. She was an excellent seamstress, and made all my clothes—she actually made my wedding gown when I got married. She knew a lot about different types of fabric, "with nap" and "without nap."

"Men are like fabric. They have nap that is woven into the fabric of their character," she would muse.

"Depending on the angle, they appear lighter or darker. Make sure to find the 'fuzzy' part of the fabric and brush it so it will lie flat; brushed the wrong way, it will stand up." And then she would giggle.

She didn't always brush my father's fabric the right way!

All couples experience ups and downs throughout their married life. It is no secret that my husband and I have had our moments of disagreement and clashes. But at the end of the day, do we care for each other enough to put the bickering aside and try to see the problem from the other person's point of view? It is easier said than done, particularly in the heat of an argument.

I was still on my soap box, and continued.

"But the bottom line is that it won't hurt to practice caring and compromise. And don't forget the importance of humor and laughter."

That was my opinion in a nutshell. I was done delivering my oratory advice!

29

Namesakes

Lucky me, I have two namesakes!

There is a cat in Montana named Manijeh. It might have moved somewhere else with the family, or it might even be dead by now!

Matt was a fellow graduate student at Northwestern University and a friend of my husband. When the two completed their studies and were awarded their PhDs, Matt got a teaching job at Montana State University, and my husband, Khosrow, joined AMAX Coal Company in Indianapolis.

Two years passed. One day I got a call from Matt's wife asking if it was okay to name their cat "Manijeh."

"We really like your name; it sounds beautiful," she said. I was flattered!

Although it sounds French, my name is purely Persian—I'm of Iranian origin. The name appears in Ferdowsi's Shahnameh (Book of Kings), epic poems that tell the history of pre-Islamic Persia. Out of curiosity, I checked my own name on Wikipedia, and came across the love story of Bijan and Manijeh, which is in Ferdowsi's Shahnameh.

I made a quick mental connection between my name and the world famous Persian cats and told her I would be delighted to have a namesake.

"What kind of a cat is it?" I asked her, just to be sure.

"Siamese," she said.

When Khosrow's secretary abruptly resigned, due to personal reasons I assume, he needed a replacement immediately.

A young man applied for the job and got it. Though he performed all the administrative and secretarial duties well, he really was an artist by profession. His specialty was oil painting. To make ends meet, he got a day job and became my husband's secretary. He worked for a couple of years, and then he and his wife moved to another state, where his art could flourish.

A year after he had left, I received a letter from him along with a photograph of one of his paintings. In the photograph, a slender woman with very short hair, wearing white pants or a skirt, stands casually against a bare door or a wall—I couldn't tell which—with one hand by her side and her left hand over her chest. He said in his letter that he named the painting "*Manijeh*," but confessed he didn't know why! He went on to say that he had sold the painting to a woman in Louisiana. I kept looking at the photo, trying to figure out if there were any similarities between me and the solitary woman in that painting.

I could find none! Did he think of me as a lonely woman? I will never know.

Somewhere in New Orleans, a woman owns a painting named "*Manijeh*."

30

My Hobby Lobby Friend

How many different ways can we make friends?

I entered the craft store Hobby Lobby with one specific mission in mind. I needed to buy some doily paper and had no time to browse. Zipping through aisles, I caught sight of a beautiful eucalyptus wreath, half price! My feet skidded on the floor as I put the brakes on my fast-moving body. How could anyone resist such a bargain? I picked up the wreath. As I looked at it a second time, I noticed how plain it was. It definitely needed something more.

I dashed over to the silk flower section. All the flowers looked beautiful, and their prices had been reduced. I was in luck. But there was a serious problem. I could not decide what type of flower would look good on this plain-looking wreath.

It proved to be a more difficult task than I had anticipated. Walking briskly up and down the silk flower aisle, I picked up and then put down a bunch of silk flowers! I couldn't decide. I doubted my own aesthetic ability and was not sure what would look good on the wreath.

Browsing the same aisle was a woman who was picking up bundles of silk flowers. She had passed me by several times. Determined to have a second opinion, I walked up to her.

"Do you think these flowers look nice on my eucalyptus wreath?" I asked with a smile.

"Absolutely not," she replied confidently shaking her head. "Come with me."

Oh boy, with that commanding tone of voice she definitely knew what she was talking about. Without a word, I followed her. In a few minutes she picked up a beautiful stem of sunflowers with two small buds and carefully explained how and where to glue them on the wreath. And I confessed right there and then, "Indeed you have picked the right flower for this wreath." By then I had totally forgotten about my hurried state, and we started talking and visiting.

I learned this talented lady, Judy was her name, and her family had recently moved to Colorado from the East Coast. She had experience arranging flowers. She was relaxed and had a pleasant disposition about her. I handed her my business card. We said goodbye and parted.

She walked away two steps, then abruptly turned around.

"What are you and your husband doing tomorrow evening? Can you come for dinner?" she inquired and then went on to say she had also invited another couple who were new in town—their children attended the same high school.

We had no plans for the next day. "We would be delighted to come, and

I will bring a dessert."

In the evening, I cheerfully asked my husband, "Guess where we are going to dinner tomorrow evening?"

"I don't have a clue," he responded. I told him about my Hobby Lobby experience.

With arched eyebrows, an incredulous look in his eyes, and a raised voice, he objected, "What? You accepted dinner invitation from a total stranger?"

I confess, I had an uneasy feeling in my stomach and my anxiety level had increased, but I defended my action. "She is really nice, and if we like her family, and you find her husband an agreeable soul, then we could become good friends."

The rest is history. My Hobby Lobby friend turned out to be a gracious hostess and a great cook. Moreover, our husbands had plenty to talk about. It was a fabulous evening, and we enjoyed meeting the other couple, MaryAnn and Harry, whom she had invited—they had recently moved to Colorado from Australia.

This all happened over twenty years ago.

Judy, my Hobby Lobby friend, went on to organize a newcomers club, which enabled all of us to enlarge our circle of friends. She organized activities and informal get-togethers—a solid network of women emerged as a result. We shared expertise, answered questions and concerns, discussed social issues, volunteered in the community, and above all had loads of fun.

I'm forever grateful for my Hobby Lobby friend.

31

The Itsy-Bitsy Spider

Experiencing an "earworm."

When my granddaughter Eliza was almost two years old, I paid the family a visit in Seattle. Eliza had just started to talk, and like most children at this age, she loved nursery rhymes. Her favorite song was "The Itsy-Bitsy Spider."

We all sang along:

> *The itsy-bitsy spider climbed up the waterspout*
>
> *Down came the rain and washed the spider out.*
>
> *Out came the sun and dried up all the rain,*
>
> *And the itsy-bitsy spider climbed up the spout again.*

Using the motions and gestures that showed the sun and the spider was tiring me out. So, all the grown-ups took turns. She was fascinated and not only listened carefully but also demanded repeat performances.

After singing "The Itsy Bitsy-Spider" over and over again, I could not get the words out of my head. On the way back to the airport, on the plane, and even while driving home, the words kept floating in my head. It was a bit annoying.

The following morning, I found myself still humming the tune while making coffee! It was beginning to irritate me. Actually, I was the one irritating myself. Why couldn't I think of a grown-up song or even a different nursery rhyme? Why in the world was I thinking so much about this tiny little spider? By mid-day, it was driving me crazy.

Suddenly, I had an epiphany!

There was a hidden message in what happened to that little spider, and it was all related to real life. That itsy-bitsy spider was teaching me something about life. We all try to climb up the "waterspouts" of life. But there are times when before we have even had a chance to get to the top, a gush of an unforeseen rain of events pushes us down. We find ourselves completely washed out, back to square one, or at the bottom of the spout!

Do we give up? No, never. Because we know the sun is going to come out, and it will dry up the rain. Things will change, and the way will be clear again. A setback is not forever. Unhappy moments, disappointments, and defeats are never permanent. Bright moments will follow, and we will be able to resume our adventure and keep climbing up the "waterspout" of life to reach our goals.

Kudos to you, my little spider!

32

Problem with Dried Herbs

Once upon a time, I used to grow herbs.

"You got any mint?" my sister, Jaleh, asked on the phone. She lived in Florida and I was in Colorado.

"Sure," I replied.

I was growing herbs in three whisky barrels. One contained only mint, and in the other two I grew different herbs and vegetables that we liked. Some years, it was basil. Another year it was sage and rosemary. And sometimes I would throw in some cucumber or zucchini seeds and let them do their own growing.

Mint doesn't need much attention. Just give it plenty of water and let the sun shine on it, and you'll have plenty to eat or dry or use in a mojito. The mint grows fast, though, which is why I confined it in a whiskey barrel.

"It is so humid here. The herbs don't dry completely," my sister continued on the phone.

"Come to Colorado. We have plenty of sunshine and dry weather," I said with a chuckle. "Don't worry, I have dried plenty, and when you come here, I will give you as much as you want," I assured her.

My sister and her husband were coming to visit us in Colorado in July. We were to take a vacation trip together to Mexico, and then they were off to California to visit their daughter and grand kids. After we hung up, I started thinking. And the more I thought, the scarier it became.

The citizens of Colorado had voted to legalize marijuana. "Weed" had become legal here, and I was reading about it in the papers. Many shops sold the stuff and advertised for candies and cookies that contained it. Pardon me, but I'm totally ignorant about this "smoking" business—I've never touched a cigarette in my life. Good or bad, there is no judgment here.

What scared me was the fact that if I gave a bag of dried mint to my sister when she was in Colorado, she would have to take it with her to Mexico, and from there carry it in her suitcase to California and then back to Florida. Although I was going to see her in a couple of weeks, I decided to mail her the dried mint.

Mailing it was no problem. I wrapped it in a plastic bag, and included a couple of small jars of homemade cherry preserves—the cherries came from my neighbor's tree—and I mailed the box to her.

She called me.

"Why did you pay so much postage to mail the mint?" she asked. I explained my reasons. She chuckled and said the thought had also occurred to her!

Now I live in Florida, and I have the same problem growing herbs. The basil becomes tall and lanky and goes to seeds; the mint produces small, thick leaves. I've killed several rosemary plants. The moral of the story is grow what does best in your climate. This is citrus country, so I've planted three different types of lemon trees. And when I mail jars of Meyer lemon marmalade to friends, I don't hesitate to let them know it is the product of my own trees!

33

My Neighbors

I've always appreciated my neighbors,
their diversity and differing views.

The exciting part of moving to a new area, at least for me, is getting to know my neighbors. No matter where we've lived in the United States, I've always enjoyed a good relationship with the folks in my neighborhood. Their differences in life-style and beliefs and getting to know and appreciate those differences, has always been thrilling to me. At one time, we had a Catholic neighbor on the right and a Mormon family on the left, and we were in the middle (we originally grew up as a Muslim). I have fond memories of that period of my life. But this is the story of two other neighbors with different perspectives on life—and we lived in Colorado at the time.

A nice family moved into the house next to us. They were devout Christian parents with two lovely little girls. A young married couple, both lawyers, had the house on the other side, and they had two beautiful large dogs.

Through neighborhood gatherings, potlucks, and games of bunco, we mingled and got to know each other well and had plenty of fun. It was at a Christmas gathering that I noticed the young couple keeping their distance. They were sitting in a corner and talking in hushed voices. She looked very unhappy, she may even have been crying. I made a mental note to check with her later to make sure she was okay.

Two days later the opportunity presented itself. We were both standing outside on the sidewalk.

"Are you okay? Is everything all right?" I asked as a mother would. I was old enough to be her mother.

"No, I had another miscarriage." She volunteered the information. She went on to say they want to start a family, but she had had several miscarriages. I didn't know that.

"Oh, I'm really sorry to hear that," I ventured delicately.

"Thank you. It is really hard," she proceeded to tell me. Then pointing to the house where my other neighbor lived, she continued. "Betty says it is the will of God. But I have certain problem that needs to be corrected. We've figured out what it is. It has nothing to do with God."

I understood where both neighbors were coming from. The young woman, highly educated and Catholic, did not appreciate the other neighbor dragging God into the situation, as if God had something to do with her multiple miscarriages. She worked on correcting the problem.

Lo and behold, in less than a year, we heard she was pregnant. The whole neighborhood was jubilant. She was huge and waddled around, and we all knew she was going to have twin girls.

Someone in the neighborhood gave a baby shower, and the cake, decorations, and all the gifts were pink. In due time, two pink storks were firmly grounded in their front yard. The babies were adorable, one blonde and the other brunette. Did God have a hand in that? Certainly whatever the problem was, the doctors had fixed it.

The doctors must have done a very good job because in less than a year she was pregnant again.

The will of God, with the husband's help, of course. The neighbors were surprised. So soon? This time they had a darling little boy.

Needless to say, the young family was ecstatic and very busy. We enjoyed having them next door. Now they had three children under the age of two. God bless the mother-in-law who showed up regularly to help out. I had the opportunity to baby sit for the children on a couple of occasions. They were such a joy! It was fun to watch them pulling a red wagon with two little girls inside and pushing the little boy in the stroller, followed by two big and well-behaved dogs—all going to the nearby park.

As fate would have it, the young man's law firm transferred him to another state. They prepared to move. The day I saw the donation truck in front of their house, I was certain they were done having children. All those beautiful Fisher-Price toys were being hauled away for needy children somewhere else. They had no problem selling their house, and then they were gone.

Almost a year later, my husband and I were travelling and passing through the state they had moved to. We stopped for a quick visit. The children remembered us—even the dogs acted friendly. It was nice to see them settled and happy, having exactly what they wanted. The young mother was radiant and glowing. The move definitely had agreed with her, I thought.

Eight months later, she gave birth to twin boys. God bless them all.

34

Entertaining Martha

Have you ever entertained Martha Stewart in your home?

We were living in Colorado. Our house guest, from Boston, was a certified professional chef who briefly owned a catering business and for a while was the online editor of a top-notch cooking magazine.

I didn't expect to be as good a cook as she was, but I do hold my own—after being on shaky cooking ground early in my married life. I have a relatively fair reputation for being a good cook. But sometimes life doesn't turn out the way you expect it.

Dinner did not turn out well. The rice, which I've cooked a thousand times with crispy *tahdig*, was not done properly and did not yield the customary golden crust at the bottom of the pan. The reason was that I started cooking the rice early, then realized the guests were arriving later than anticipated. My husband, Khosrow, turned the burners off and the rice sat there until we turned the heat back on again. This is a cardinal sin when it comes to cooking rice Persian style. It is temperamental and does not do well if one doesn't keep the temperature steady and even.

The homemade guacamole, for some odd reason, became rather liquidy as if it had too much lime juice in it. Too much chopped tomato, perhaps? I don't know!

One can't fuss too much about cooking simple green beans. Those nice firm beans are easy to boil in hot water, toss with some butter and crumbled bacon bits, and top with toasted sliced almonds. Having seen how professionals grab a pinch of kosher salt from a bowl—and I did have kosher salt—I decided to use it instead of my usual salt shaker. However, my pinch must have been different in size; the beans came out incredibly salty. This was especially embarrassing because earlier I had announced to everyone, "We have cut back on salt."

I humbly confess that my chocolate éclairs are rather well-known among friends. Then why on earth didn't I make them for this occasion? I'll never know! I had ordered a pumpkin roll from a neighborhood kid to support her school. The roll arrived the same day as our company. I decided to serve that for dessert. Big mistake! The filling was super sweet and the roll itself was rather dry. I kept offering to put a scoop of vanilla ice-cream on top, but no one seemed interested.

The dinner disaster, in my mind, had to be compensated by a good hearty breakfast. Fresh strawberries and blueberries would be the perfect accompaniment to nice fluffy pancakes, and an assortment of syrups. The only problem was my self-rising flour decided not to rise that morning. I have never produced such lousy pancakes in my life. They remained flat and hard.

I pray the memory of my unprofessional meals will be over-shadowed by the visits to the Red Rocks Amphitheatre, the Garden of the Gods, and the Dinosaur Ridge, the places we managed to take our visitors from Boston. Surely, the gorgeous mountains of Colorado, combined with the geology lessons provided by Khosrow must have compensated for the lousy food!

35

Islam and Christianity

What do I really believe in?

When Carl, a friend from the church I attend, asked me to speak on Islam, my husband looked at me and asked, "Do you consider yourself a Muslim?"

That was a very good question, one that I had asked myself over and over again. I had come to the conclusion that my view on Islam was strictly unique and personal and that I had been able to fuse it with a Christian framework. So, what was I really? A Muslim or a Christian?

I grew up in Iran in a Muslim household. Of the two major sects of Islam, Shiite and Sunnis, the majority of Iranians are Shiite. My family happened to be Shiite. Years later I married a young man who grew up in a Sunni family. It was like a Protestant and Catholic marrying each other—both believing in Christianity.

We are all products of our environment and the values we are taught.

When I came to the United States and made this country my permanent home, I did not find discrepancies between the values that were ingrained in me when I was growing up, and the life and beliefs of good Christian families I met.

The core values of Islam were the basis for my upbringing: believe in a merciful God and a higher power, don't forget the power of prayer, be thankful for what you have been given, don't forget the less fortunate and contribute to charity, feel for the hungry, and do your share by giving alms with love and respect. Aren't all these the same as Christianity and what Jesus teaches us—to be socially responsible and take care of the needy in our communities?

Living in the United States, a country with diverse cultures, allowed me to look for ways to combine all those values in a modern society. Amazingly, I came to realize the core values of humanity and being a good person in Islam, are compatible and in perfect harmony with values in a good Christian or a good Jew.

The biblical principles related to ethics and worship are fundamental to Judaism, Christianity, and Islam. And that is what I had been taught. No wonder my father kept repeating there is no difference in praying in a mosque, synagogue, temple, or a church. The emphasis was on keeping God's presence in one's life, regardless of where one lived or worshiped.

So, to answer my husband's question, I would say, I'm both, a Muslim and a Christian—and I'm comfortable praying in all houses of worship.

36

For the Love of Coffee

How far would you go to find your favorite coffee?

"Nordic Jumping Beans, Steamboat Coffee Roasters." That was the label on the attractive blue bag of complementary coffee beans left in our nice resort in Steamboat Springs, Colorado. We were having a family reunion.

For two days, no one paid any attention to the bag of coffee—we used our own beans, ground them every morning, and brewed the coffee in the French press. We had some coffee snobs among us who had come from Seattle. Nothing but the best for them!

On the third day, I ventured and looked closely at the complementary coffee beans. I gingerly opened the bag, sniffed the coffee, and brewed a pot. Wow! The taste and aroma were incredible. Our group took a closer look at the bag.

"What are Nordic Jumping Beans?" someone asked.

The answer was right on the bag, in small letters: "It is a signature recipe of hand-picked beans, creating a lighter full-bodied roast, the perfect collection from Brazil, Sumatra Guatemala, Mexico, and Columbia." That is why it delivered such a smooth coffee experience!

Now we were on a mission to find Steamboat Coffee Roasters. Our first stop was at the concierge desk at the resort.

"Where can we buy some more of this coffee?" I asked Nancy, the concierge.

She laughed and asked, "Did you like it?"

"Of course, we did! Can we pick up some at the local grocery store?"

"I doubt it, but you're welcome to check," she replied.

I narrowed my eyes and asked, "Can we go directly to the roasting place?" I was pretty sure if we went to the source, we could buy some.

Nancy gave us the directions and drew a map and said it was across from a beer distribution outfit, past the downtown area. Armed with this information, we piled into the car, determined to find the Steamboat Coffee Roasters. After all, how difficult could it be? It was just across from the beer delivery place!

Big trucks leaving the beer distribution plant were hard to miss. So, we all looked at the opposite side of the road to find the roasting place. Nothing! Just a few private homes, and they did not resemble anything close to a coffee roasting place. We drove up and down the street. We came back to the beer distribution place again, but this time we drove slowly, looking at every possible building.

It occurred to me that we were all women, not stubborn or shy like men, so we could ask for directions! I stopped the car. My sister, Jaleh, jumped out and spoke with a man standing in front of his mechanic shop. They exchanged a few words, and Jaleh came back quickly.

"He says we didn't go far enough." "We are to look to our right. If we see the 'tin man,' we've gone too far." The coffee roasting place was tucked in the back. "Moreover," my sister continued, "we should be able to smell the coffee if they are roasting it."

We drove slowly. As soon as we spotted the shiny "tin man," the metal structure, all of us stretched our necks to the right. I think it was my daughter-in-law, Kate, who yelled, "There it is!" We drove on a short gravel road, and there on our right was a small, unassuming building: Steamboat Coffee Roasters. So, this is where they roasted that delicious coffee!

We walked in.

A blonde, attractive petite woman in her forties greeted us with a huge smile. We learned her name was Angie Robinson and that she owned the place. We shared with her our adventure of trying to find her place and the fact that we loved her coffee so much we had to come for more.

Angie provided samples to all the resorts in the area and basically sold wholesale and shipped all over the United States. She was done with the roasting for that day and had sent her helpers home, thinking no one would be calling at the end of the day. But we did, and our persistence paid off.

We had Angie all to ourselves, and she gave us a tour of the place. We learned about the different types of beans and where they came from. She showed us the roaster and basically gave us a lesson in coffee roasting. Angie was a delightful person and talked about her coffee business with a sense of pride and glee. It was obvious that she loved her line of work. I wondered if her genuine enthusiasm and love for her coffee spilled into the roasting process— maybe that is what we experienced with each cup of her coffee!

We left the Steamboat Coffee Roasters with bags of coffee beans under our arms.

37

Fruitcake

When was the last time you made fruitcake?

I've stopped making fruitcakes. That doesn't mean I don't like to eat them. I just don't make them any-more. In my earlier baking days, I loved making this holiday specialty using bright red and green candied cherries, plump raisins, candied lemon and orange peels, tons of pecans, molasses, and spices—a real traditional fruitcake.

Once, I tasted a fruitcake that was totally different.

In graduate school, a professor invited us over for a bit of holiday cheer. His wife, Mary, had made lemon fruitcake. As the name indicates, it had intense lemon flavor. I asked for the recipe. She gave it to me and added that it had come from Phoebe Sherwood. (I never knew who Phoebe Sherwood was.) I took the recipe and promptly filed it in my recipe box. Many years passed, but then one Christmas, I took Phoebe Sherwood's recipe out of the box and tried it. It called for a large bottle of lemon flavoring, the entire bottle! I never made that recipe again.

One Christmas, I was visiting my son and his family in Seattle. My daughter-in-law, Kate, had picked up the tradition and made a lovely, delicious, dense fruitcake. Not only did I eat my fill, I also cut a couple of slices, put them in a plastic bag, and tucked them in my purse. I needed something to go with my Seattle Starbucks coffee at the airport on the way back home to Colorado.

At the airport, I went through the security as usual. But then I was asked to put my purse on the belt one more time. I did.

"Would you mind putting your purse on the belt again?" the officer asked politely. I was surprised, but I didn't mind. The purse went through the X-ray a second time.

"Ma'am, would you please step aside?" the security officer asked. He wanted to examine the contents of my purse. Without hesitation, I cheerfully complied.

The security officer unzipped my shoulder bag and started rummaging through the contents. Then, he picked up the plastic bag containing the two thick slices of fruitcake, brought the plastic bag close to his face, narrowed his eyes, and asked, "What is this?"

"Oh, that is a wonderful fruitcake my daughter-in-law made for Christmas," I said. "It is dense and very delicious. Would you like to have a piece?"

"I don't mind if I do," the officer replied with a charming smile. I graciously offered him the whole bag. Equally as gracious, he accepted my offer and grinning from ear to ear, announced that he would eat it right away.

It was heartwarming to observe that someone else liked fruitcake as much as I did. While I was sipping my coffee before boarding the plane, I wondered if the fruitcake was safe for him to eat, having gone through the X-ray machine several times!

38

How to Eat Pastries

I wrote this story for Ali, with whom I shared the joy of eating pastries!

A big box of delicious-looking pastries is on the kitchen table; somebody has removed the top.

Ali and I walk into the kitchen and nonchalantly glance at the open box. A few round tartlets with glazed fruit on top—peaches and plums—they look tantalizing.

Small rectangular two-layered sponge cakes, put together with whipped cream and jam and dusted with cocoa powder, look absolutely inviting. A few cream puffs are tucked in the corners of the box. Some are covered with chocolate ganache, and a couple are simply dusted with powdered sugar. Smack in the middle of the box are two delicate-looking *mille-feuilles,* which I call napoleons. We eye those two, but politeness dictates that we be considerate of others. We are well-mannered.

As weight-conscious as we both are, neither one of us wants to be the first to grab a piece. We try to act nonchalant and curb our intense desire to eat those pastries. After a minute of idle-talk, I suggest we share one *mille-feuille*. Ali nods approvingly. This suits us well because it doesn't make us look greedy. We get a small plate and a sharp knife and cut the napoleon right in the middle, causing some of the cream to ooze out.

We each meticulously pick up a half. But it does not take long before we shove it into our mouths and swallow it. What did we think? It was only a half of a napoleon, and the brains are not satisfied. Again, we look at each other, and coyly agree that we need to share another *mille-feuille* as if eating two halves is eating less than one whole! We share a second one.

The rest of the family, busy talking in the living-room, does not know what is going on in the kitchen. Another minute goes by.

Comfortable with our philosophy of eating only a half, we decide to share one of the rectangular pastries—it is really light because it is sponge cake. Delicious! It goes down very quickly.

What a shame not to taste the tartlets! One in particular topped with fruit and a shiny glaze is amazingly beautiful. You guessed it, we carefully cut it in half. Ali and I are not fussy about who gets which half. I end up with the peach half, and Ali gets the plum.

Now our brains are totally satisfied, and we feel content.

"I wonder how the plum tastes!" I blurt out.

Ali nods in agreement and says, "I was also wondering how the peach tastes!"

At this point, the rest of the family walks in, and we offer them what is left in the box.

39

At the Airport

Similarities in life never cease to amaze me!

Lufthansa Flight 446 from Frankfurt has landed in Denver. My husband and I pace the floor as the passengers slowly walk out of the big double door.

I'm worried about my mother who is going through the customs and immigration all by herself. She is in her eighties and does not speak a word of English. How is she going to handle the custom formalities? Will she be able to ask for help? Can she ask someone to lift her suitcases? No doubt it will take her longer to clear customs. Her age combined with her language problem make me nervous and worried.

I ask my husband to keep watch while I dash to the restroom. When I return, I see him talking to a tall, gorgeous blonde girl. She is in her early twenties, has a beautiful body, and is wearing a blouse that shows her midriff. As I approach them, my husband turns to me.

"This young lady needs to make a call and doesn't know where to find a public phone."

I look at her. She smiles, and I wonder why among all these people she asked my husband!

"Where do you want to call?" I inquire.

She pulls out a faxed sheet of paper and shows me a number, area code 425, state of Washington.

"Would you like to make a collect call?" I ask and point to the two phone booths near where we are standing.

"Collect?" she repeats and adds "Need phone card. Where to buy?"

It doesn't take me long to realize she does not speak much English. Since the flight has arrived from Germany, I assume she speaks German.

"Sind Sie von Deutschland?"

"Nein. Von Russland" she replies softly.

I turn to my husband. "Oh, she is Russian." I pull out my cell phone and hand it to her.

"Here, you can use my phone to make your call." Then I add, "Give me your number, I'll dial it for you. Who do you want to speak with?"

"Jasmine" she replies.

I dial the numbers, and a receptionist answers at the other end. It must be a place of business.

"Hello. May I speak with Jasmine, please?"

"Who is calling?"

"I'm at the Denver International Airport. A young lady by the name of Olga wishes to speak with Jasmine."

"Oh, just a moment please."

At this point I hand the phone to Olga and put distance between us so she can speak freely. I keep glancing at the custom's door. A knot is forming in my stomach. Where is my mother?

Olga finishes her conversation and gives me back the phone.

"Jasmine says call again. Ten minutes," she says in broken English.

We both walk toward the phone booths. I try to explain how to make a collect call. A momentary thought crosses my mind: to be young and adventurous, to arrive in a foreign country, not able to speak the language with no one waiting at the airport to greet you. But isn't that what my mother is doing at her old age? Except I'm at the airport and worried sick! I hope nothing goes wrong and she gets through the immigration okay.

I check my watch. Has it been ten minutes yet? "Do you want to call Jasmine back?" I ask and press the number showing on my cell phone. The same receptionist answers. Olga talks again and returns the phone. Still keeping an eye on the passenger arrival door, I ask Olga where she is headed.

"Beufer, Durango," she says. I can only comprehend Durango.

Why on earth is she going to Durango?

"Are you a student?" I ask.

"In Russia, yes."

"What will you do in Durango?"

"I have paper to work there," she says.

I do not inquire further into the nature of her job. She then shows me the faxed sheet again and points to a second number she wants to call. I dial and hear an answering machine.

I hand Olga the cell phone. "Here, leave a message because they are not home."

I'm worried about Mother; why isn't she out of customs yet?

"Need Greyhound bus to Durango." Olga points to the words on the paper.

Goodness gracious, helping this young lady is getting to be a bit complicated.

"Olga, wait here. I will find someone who can help you." I see a uniformed airport officer turning around the corner. I run to catch up with him.

"Sir!" I shout. He turns around. "I need your help."

The officer says calmly but with a frown, "What is the problem? What can I do for you?"

"Please come with me," I say. He follows me, looking not too pleased, but rather annoyed. I'm probably cutting into his break time. We both walk back to where Olga is standing. She smiles, a very pretty and charming smile. The officer's disposition softens immediately, and his thick eyebrows untie themselves. I explain the situation. Olga repeats that she needs to get to Durango on Greyhound bus.

"Okay," says the officer kindly. "I'm going to take her to customer service and they can help her get to where she needs to go." They walk away and I feel relieved.

Relief turns to curiosity and more anxiety. I'm curious about what Olga will be doing in Durango and anxious for her to arrive safely at her destination; I'm also curious about what is going on behind closed doors at the customs office, and anxious to see my mother.

Within five minutes, Mother shows up in a wheelchair, smiling from ear to ear and deep in a highly animated conversation with a young black man who is pushing the wheelchair with one hand, and pulling her suitcase with the other. He is laughing and talking with my mother like two old friends who just found each other after a long separation! I gaze at her almost speechless. I'm amazed at her ability to communicate!

My anxiety melts away and my body relaxes. Mother is here and she looks happy. No doubt Olga, too, will make it to Durango safely.

40

A Day at the Auction

My husband and I had never been to an auction.
But there is a first time for everything.

Phoebe and Jim, our good friends, introduce us to a new experience—attending an auction.

The sight of all the merchandise, wherever it came from, and the fast-talking auctioneers get us all excited. We are amazed at the variety of pieces of furniture and household goods for sale, not to mention all the free coffee, donuts, and hot dogs one can have! We learn how to show interest in an item by holding up the number that was assigned to us when we arrived. For some reason, my husband feels the urge to buy something, anything. We end up with a wrought iron structure—similar to a baker's rack—for which we have absolutely no use, nor do we have a place to put it. Frankly, we can do without this piece, but it is fun to buy something! We put the rack in the garage for the time being until we figure out what to do with it.

Then my mother comes for a visit from Iran.

She has never been to an auction either, and I'm eager to show her how items from old estates are bought and sold in the United States. My husband absolutely refuses to accompany us; he says he has a fear of "buying on impulse," and prefers to stay at home. I pride myself for not acting on impulse and have no intention of buying anything—the whole purpose is to show my mother how an auction is conducted. Jim and Phoebe pick us up.

Mother and I browse. She eats a hot dog, and I have a cup of coffee. Phoebe takes delight in showing my mother all the merchandise, and then we come across several huge hand-made rugs.

"How ridiculous is it for me to even get close to these rugs! I have plenty of Persian rugs at home," I casually comment to Mother.

"It doesn't hurt to look," she says while biting into her hot dog.

She narrows her eyes, and examines one of the rugs closely. It is definitely a Persian design, with crimson borders and a medallion in the middle, and it is semi-folded. Mother keeps looking at it. Finally, when the auctioneer fully displays the rug on the floor, Mother turns to me.

"You should bid on this one."

I cannot believe what I'm hearing.

"But Mom, I don't need one," I protest.

"It will look very nice in your living room," she whispers. "Look at the medallion and the design," she says with conviction.

She knows—she has lived with Persian rugs all her life and is knowledgeable about colors and designs. Her own mother—my grandmother—had a carpet weaving facility in her home when my mother was a little girl. I'm told my grandmother hired a husband and wife who were full-time weavers and produced two or three rugs for her each year.

Like an obedient child, I listen to her and raise my number. I feel anxious. What will my husband say? I'm worried about his reaction.

Another hand goes up. A sense of relief comes over me. I'm off the hook. As the auctioneer announces the new price, Mother grabs my elbow and literally shoves my hand up into the air. I'm bidding again.

I end up buying that huge Persian rug!

My mother's enthusiasm about this particular rug is contagious. However, the euphoria of owning a genuine Persian rug is immediately replaced by the anxiety of how to break the news to Khosrow! My solid reputation for not buying on impulse is tarnished forever! Particularly since I bought an item we absolutely do not need.

Flanked by my mother and our good friends, Phoebe and Jim, I ring the doorbell with trembling hands. My husband opens the door immediately. Jim bravely walks in ahead of us, and without any introduction whatsoever, announces the purchase of the rug, and hastily adds it was at a bargain price!

"It is a Tabriz, beautiful crimson color with a medallion," Mother chimes in.

Faced with a done deal, my husband only shakes his head. We bring the rug in.

My mother is mighty pleased with herself for not letting her daughter pass up a good deal.

I never went back to that auction house again.

41

World's Best Key Lime Pie

Delicious and worth the wait, for sure!

We moved to Florida and are new to the area, but we have managed to find a shortcut that takes us to a big shopping center. This shortcut goes through residential areas and is used by many locals. Once in a while, I notice signs posted along the side of the road that announce, "World's best key lime pie, sold on Friday, at 11 a.m."

I've seen such signs several times since we moved a year ago. I am curious about the pie, but never manage to be on that road on a Friday at 11 a.m.

But today, I am on that road! And here is the story of the world's best key lime pie.

It is 10:15 a.m., and I'm driving home from my exercise class—I'm determined to lose two more pounds! It dawns on me that it is Friday and that I had seen the pie sign yesterday. Voila! I head for the shortcut.

It is 10:25 by now.

As I reach a vast empty field, I see four cars already lined up on one side. I roll the window down and ask an older gentleman, "Is this the line for the key lime pie?" He looks at me with no expression on his face.

"Yes, it is," he says nonchalantly.

"Is the pie really good?" I ask with a smile.

"Yes, it is," he replies calmly.

"Then I must get to the back of the line?" I ask, feeling rather stupid.

"If you want to buy the pie," he says looking at me as if I'm a moron.

I drive to the back of the line—now there are six cars ahead of me.

While waiting in the car, I pull out my cell phone and call my husband. "Can you guess where I am?" I ask jubilantly.

"I don't have the foggiest notion," he says, with a tinge of curiosity in his voice.

"I'm in line to buy that famous key lime pie."

"Wow, I thought we were trying to lose weight," he protests with a chuckle.

"Yes, but we have to taste this pie at least once, and it is close to 11 a.m." I look at my watch, it is 10:43. We hang up.

Next, I call my sister:

"Can you guess where I am right now?" I know she's smiling at the other end as she says she doesn't have a clue. My family knows me well!

"I'm in line to buy a key lime pie. Would you like me to pick up one for you?" I ask.

"Good heavens, no!" she says laughing out loud. "We don't eat dessert. Besides, you are buying one, and we will come over to taste it."

The cars are arriving one after another, lining up on empty grassy field or parking on the side of the road. It is almost 11:00, and I notice folks are getting out of their cars and lining up somewhere in the middle of the field. I do the same, and walk fast to get in line.

There are twenty people standing in line ahead of me waiting for the truck to arrive! By now, I am counting about sixty-five cars.

Then, a short, slender, middle-aged man walks onto the field, directing traffic and telling those folks who have parked in the path of the truck to move their cars. This is done in an orderly manner. Then a young man shows up. Both men put on a white apron and a chef's hat. The names on the apron read Rob and Tim, the older and the younger one, respectively.

It is beastly hot, probably close to 90 degrees with high humidity. But everyone is waiting patiently.

People are holding their money—a twenty-dollar bill—that is how much each pie costs. *It better be good for that price.*

The line curves, and now there are roughly seventy folks behind me. Everyone is looking to see if the truck is arriving. I walk over to Rob and start asking questions about this whole operation.

"Anthony is the baker," Rob says. "He has been making these key lime pies for the past twenty-five years and selling them here in this field for the past seven years." Rob tells me all about these wonderful pies. "Anthony uses only four ingredients: eggs, milk, sugar, and key lime juice in a special graham cracker crust." Rob appears to be the marketing man for Anthony's business. I also learn that Anthony delivers pies to customers' homes, at no additional charge.

It is sweltering hot, and I'm perspiring profusely.

The white truck arrives. A big sign in front says "Family Owned and God Blessed." The truck parks where it is supposed to, and I get to see Anthony, who broadly smiles as he gets out of the truck, opens the back of the truck, and pulls down a ramp. I see four large chest freezers in there. *The pies are all frozen.* Anthony brings out a cooler and tells folks to help themselves to cold bottled-water. Then a radio is put on a small folding table, and music floats in the air.

Anthony greets the customers, assuring everyone that his kitchen is certified and that he is licensed to do business. Tim and Rob take trays of samples around. I get my first little taste of the world's best key lime pie. Absolutely delicious!

The line is moving, and I find myself in front of Anthony, ready to be handed a pie. When he puts a frozen pie in a bag for me, I coyly say, "Two pies, please!"

Anthony assures me it keeps in the freezer for a month, but I know it will be consumed way before the month ends.

42

For the Love of Ginger

Oh, the things we learn in life, and how quickly we learn them!

"We are taking a vacation and will be out of town for a week" my son said on the phone.

"If you want, I'm available to come and stay with Eliza while you are gone, I offered. I lived in Colorado at the time and they were in Seattle.

"Oh, that will be very nice," my son cheerfully accepted.

My granddaughter is a beautiful, smart, responsible, and self-sufficient junior in high school. She is vegan and does her own cooking. She drives herself to school and yoga practices. She does not need a grown-up around. But I felt it would be a great opportunity for the two of us, particularly me, to have some time together—bonding time between a grandma and her granddaughter. I arrived a day before her parents left for vacation.

"Ginger is sick and needs to take medication," said my daughter-in-law, Kate. Then she showed me how to put the pill inside the treat and give it to Ginger, their dog.

Ginger was a mellow, quiet, black German shepherd and Aussie mix. She moved around the kitchen slowly and mostly slept. I never heard her bark. I got the instructions on how much food and water to give Ginger, although I was told it was Eliza's dog and her responsibility.

The following morning, with everyone gone, it was Ginger and me. Medication, food, water, letting her out—I followed the instructions I was given. Truth be told, I never had a dog growing up, and never knew how to take care of one. The closest experience of having an animal in the house was the occasional alley cats that roamed around the pool at my grandfather's house in Tehran.

Eliza came home from school and promptly went to her room to do her homework. It was Friday evening and she was to go out with her friends later. Ginger curled up in her cushion and seemed too lethargic for any kind of activity.

It was a beautiful early evening in that suburb of Seattle. I decided to take a walk around the neighborhood after dinner. Making sure all the doors and windows were properly closed and locked, with my cell phone in hand, I let myself out through the garage—I was given the garage door code number.

I walked for more than half an hour, breathing in the lovely fresh air and admiring all the flowers and the greenery in that beautiful neighborhood. When I returned and stepped into the garage, I realized I had locked myself out—I had locked the door that led to the house from the garage!

No problem. Eliza surely has a key to the house. I sent her a text message.

"No, I don't have a key because the front door is always unlocked when I come home," she responded.

Surely my son and his wife must have a spare key somewhere in the garage! I called them.

No, they didn't keep a spare key anywhere, and none of the neighbors kept a key to their house either! *Good grief. What do I do now?*

"You have no choice but to call a locksmith," my son suggested.

Not knowing much about the area, I walked to the neighbor's house to get help in finding a locksmith. A young gentleman opened the door with two little girls in tow. They were in their pajamas and ready for bed.

"Sorry to bother you. I'm the grandmother next door, and I'm afraid I've done something stupid—I've locked myself out. May I use a phone book to locate a locksmith?" I said sheepishly.

At that precise moment I received a text message from my son with the phone number for a locksmith. The gracious neighbor asked his wife to take the kids to bed and called the locksmith on my behalf and walked out with me to keep me company in the garage until the locksmith arrived.

Two experts showed up within half an hour. Without further ado, they informed me it would cost $175 to unlock the door. Heeding the plea from a little old lady for a reduced fee, they agreed to take $125, if I paid cash. I agreed!

In less than ten minutes, they opened the door. I paid all the cash I had, thanked the neighbor, and walked into the house. It was 10:00 p.m.

Shortly thereafter Eliza, who was oblivious to what had happened, walked in.

"My friends were wondering if you and I were going to sleep in the car in the garage tonight!" she said laughing and promptly went to her room to sleep.

So did I—I was physically and emotionally exhausted.

It was very early in the morning when I felt movement near my bed. With half-opened eyes, I saw Ginger standing in the middle of the room looking at me. Poor dog, she must be hungry and wants her food, I thought. Then I noticed. There was a huge puddle on the rug and a bigger mess on the stairs. I had forgotten to let Ginger out last night!

"Eliza, honey, can you help me?" I yelled out. But there was no response from the sleeping teenager.

Suffice to say, with gloves on, I spent hours cleaning up the rug, the stairs, and everything else in between. I felt extremely bad and sorry for Ginger. She actually had not been let out since I went for my walk yesterday afternoon. Ginger was now my responsibility. I quickly learned how to take care of a dog. Nothing teaches you like experience! From then on, for the duration of my stay, I made sure to take the house key with me and walk Ginger around the neighborhood twice a day. The dog and I bonded.

The day after the locked-door episode, while walking Ginger, the neighbor's two little girls were out riding their tricycles in their driveway. The older one waived and yelled, "Hello, stupid grandmother," at which point the father lunged to admonish the girl.

I laughed heartily and then knelt by the little girl, who was still sitting on her tricycle looking bewildered.

"Honey, I'm not stupid. I made a mistake," I told her with a smile. "If I repeat the same mistake again, then I'm stupid." She looked at me with wide eyes and a cute smile and nodded approvingly.

In a crash course, I learned how to take care of a dog, and truly bonded with Ginger.

Because of her old age and incurable sickness, Ginger was put to rest a few months later.

43

The Taj Mahal

Shohreh and I have known each other since 1961 when we were both high school exchange students in the United States.

I'm visiting my mother in Tehran. I connect with my long-time friend, Shohreh. She invites me to join her family and a group of friends for dinner at an Indian restaurant in an upscale neighborhood in Tehran. She gives me the address and adds that the restaurant is well-known and all cab drivers know exactly where it is located.

The cabbie who picks me up in front of Mother's house happens to be an old gentleman—the religious kind with a beard and worry beads hanging from the rearview mirror, and he is playing a Quran recitation on his radio. This is a different experience from my previous cab rides when the cabbies usually crank up modern songs—happy music.

"The Taj Mahal restaurant, please," I announce calmly and with confidence.

"Sorry, I don't know where that is," he says while looking at me in the rearview mirror. I get worried but reply casually, "No problem, I have the address." We drive on.

As we get closer to the vicinity of where the place should be, he stops the car and says he needs to check the address with somebody else. He jumps out of the car and goes into a small grocery store to ask for the exact location. For some reason, my address is not sufficient for him!

"The restaurant is not far. All I have to do is go to the next light, turn left, and go straight two blocks, and Taj Mahal would be on the right; easy enough," he reports back his findings.

He drives on.

I see an ornate building with people streaming out, each carrying a Styrofoam container. Men and children are pouring out of the building. *This must be a popular family restaurant. Everyone is carrying their leftovers.* The building has plenty of beautiful tile work up the front of it. The cabbie says this is the Taj Mahal. I'm not familiar with the streets and places in Tehran, so I believe him, pay and step out.

I sense something odd as I approach the building. The women who come out are all wearing black traditional chador, a head covering. Then I observe something even stranger about this restaurant—the entrance is segregated, one for men and the other for women! I don't think much of it because after the Islamic revolution, Iran adopted gender segregation in public places. I head for the entrance designated by a sign saying "Sisters." A huge colorful Persian rug is hanging like a curtain in front of the entrance. In a flash, I remember a dinner we had at a Moroccan restaurant in Denver, Mataam Fez, which used the same concept of hanging carpets from the walls.

I lift the carpet and walk in. I have to climb up the stairs, but a steady stream of women all covered in black chador are coming down—like a one-way traffic. *This is rather strange. Why did Shohreh, who resides permanently in Los Angeles and is in Tehran to visit her ailing mother, choose such a restaurant to entertain friends? It doesn't jive with her style!*

The stairs are rather narrow, and with all the ladies coming down, it is pretty difficult to move against the crowd.

"You are late. It is finished," a woman suddenly volunteers to inform me. *I'm confused.*

"What do you mean it is finished? This is the time my friend asked me to come. Isn't this the Taj Mahal?" I am surprised and irked. I am late only by 15 minutes, and by Iranian standards, it is not late at all.

"What? This is no Taj Mahal. This is a mosque," the woman replies curtly.

Oops! The cab driver and his lack of knowledge about the Taj Mahal created an embarrassing situation for me. I sheepishly turn around to retrace my steps when I hear a young woman's voice from behind, "The Taj Mahal is just around the next corner." I walk out, and with brisk steps proceed toward the next block.

No wonder people were carrying food—it was *Arbaeen,* the fortieth day of the slaying of Imam Ali, a Shia-revered religious martyr and son-in-law of the Prophet Muhammad. That is the day when mosques traditionally distribute food among the needy.

44

Mancho, the Cab Driver

One afternoon, at the height of rush hour in Tehran, I took my mother to her dentist to have a tooth extracted.

He preferred to be called Mancho, though his real name was Manouchehr. He was the cab driver who took us to Dr. Jafari, my mother's dentist, whose new office was on the northern part of Tehran.

Mancho was a lively and talkative soul. As he maneuvered through the crowded streets in Tehran, he kept us entertained by telling us his life story. Right after the Iranian Revolution, he had fled to Rome, Italy. But after several months, he had opted to come back, "Because I was happier in my own homeland and truly missed my family, especially my grandmother," he said with a big smile.

His base of operation was the northern part of Tehran, near Tajrish and Vanak, and that is the reason he was well familiar with that part of the city and knew all the side streets and back alleys and could bypass the traffic during the rush hour.

Dr. Jafari's office was located on a one-way street. Bravely and with no qualms, Mancho entered this one-way street from the opposite side. I closed my eyes and whispered a prayer. Mancho smiled broadly and kept apologizing to the drivers of the oncoming cars. To my amazement, they were all gracious and let him pass. We reached the doctor's office, safely!

Mancho offered to wait for us while Mother was having her tooth extracted. We gladly accepted his offer because securing a return cab would have been close to impossible at that time of the day. This meant Mancho had time to find himself a nice parking spot right in front of the doctor's building while listening to his beloved soccer game on the car radio.

My mother was Dr. Jafari's first patient that afternoon, and she was immediately ushered into the operating room. I waited and watched as other patients arrived.

Suddenly the door to the waiting room flung open, a harried and frazzled man walked in with a member of his family—I assumed it was his wife. He quickly mumbled something about having parked illegally and dashed out. By this time, Mother had come out of the operating room, and I was given instructions on how to take care of her for the next few days.

We walked out of the building and proceeded toward our waiting cab. When Mancho told the frazzled man that we were leaving and that he could have the parking spot, I witnessed an incredible scene. Never had I seen a happier man. It was as if he had just been handed a winning lottery ticket. His joy was so profound that he hugged Mancho and started kissing him on both cheeks and would not let go! Parking spots are hard to find in that area, and I figured the horrible traffic contributed to the man's nervousness and drove him a bit crazy!

I was equally nervous about Mother's dental surgery. Not only she was diabetic, she also had had heart bypass surgery a couple of years prior. But the extraction was successful, and a hearty chicken soup and a nice banana milkshake soon put her on the road to a quick recovery.

Mancho deserved the "Man of the Week" award, and I truly appreciated his help.

All's well that ends well.

45

The Good Doctor

It is a joy to meet people who truly love their profession and derive a
deep satisfaction from it despite its daily ups and downs. I met such
a person, a mild-mannered medical doctor who told me stories about
his past experiences after completing medical school. His first job as
a young physician was in a small, remote town, somewhere in the
northwest of Iran. This is his story.

He received his free medical education at the University of Tehran. As a payback, the government assigned him to a small remote town, northwest of Iran, to serve folks who did not have a doctor in their town. He was young and fresh out of medical school. He became a country doctor, practicing all the routine stuff, including delivering babies. However, he sent the complicated cases to a nearby city hospital. He worked hard and seldom took a day off. He enjoyed serving people and became a well-known person in that town.

A family member advised him to take at least one day off and explore the country side. So, he did, going out of town on a one-day excursion while his uncle drove the car. He enjoyed the sight of the green hills and valleys. Driving through a small, remote village in the mountains, they noticed a group of villagers huddled near the road talking among themselves. As soon as they saw a car approaching, they flagged it down. The uncle got out of the car and approached the group to find out what the problem was.

"We have a pregnant lady in labor. It appears to be a hard delivery, too much for the local midwife to handle," a man said. "We want to take her to that well-known doctor in the next town, but we have no transportation to get her there," the man lamented.

Upon hearing the man's request and the mention of his nephew's name, the uncle smiled broadly.

"No need to take her to that town. I brought you the doctor, and he is right here in the car!" The doctor was exactly where he was needed to be, even on his day off.

He delivered the baby and all was well.

The good doctor, who is now a prominent urologist in private practice in Tehran as well as a clinical professor of medicine, continued with the story.

One afternoon thirty years later, a young woman stepped into his office. She inquired if the doctor had ever been to a particular remote village. When the doctor told her he had been there, the young woman said, "I'm the baby you delivered 30 years ago. My mother had told me the whole story, and now that I'm in Tehran, I wanted to meet you."

When the good doctor told me this story, he was crying; so was I. No doubt he enjoyed sharing the story with me. He is in his seventies now, but the love for his profession and the satisfaction he draws from helping people have not diminished a bit. What a gem of a doctor! How lucky are his patients and my mother who had him as a neighbor.

46

Obituary

I once had my college students write my obituary.

I taught educational psychology at Boise State University after I earned my doctorate.

The course I taught, TE225, was offered through the teacher education program and was a requirement for teacher certification in Idaho. Consequently, in addition to the usual undergraduates who were getting a degree in education, I had many students who already had a college degree and wanted to get a teaching certificate in order to teach their respective fields, like science, literature, or art.

Teaching is both an art and a science, and I was thrilled to have the opportunity to utilize my creativity in engaging my adult students. Lecturing to a large group with various backgrounds made me feel like an actor on stage entertaining the audience! I planned every lesson carefully in order to keep them alert and on their toes so they would not yawn and go to sleep. And that was no easy task, particularly when it came to my Saturday morning class—three hours straight! I assume the college set it up that way so those who had jobs during the week could still attend and earn their teaching certificate.

It was April of 1995 and time for the final assessment. Students had requested, and I granted their wish, to have a writing assignment. It was an essay-type MRI, written in class. I never used the word *"test."* I preferred MRI—Mental Registration Index—a rose is still a rose by any other name! I needed to register how much information they had retained, and what they had learned in my class. I gave them the following writing assignment:

You are reading the local newspaper. You come to the obituary section, and a name catches your eyes. You read that Manijeh Badiozamani passed away at the age of 95 of natural causes. You say to yourself, "I remember her—we called her Dr. B. and I took her Saturday morning Ed. Psych class."

Now, let your memory and knowledge guide you.

- *What do you remember about this teacher's class?*
- *What did she teach? (content)*
- *How did she teach? (method of instruction)*
- *What sort of impression did she leave behind?*
- *What did you personally learn in that class? (content and theory)*

Be honest and truthful. Remember, she is dead and is not looking for flattery!

Your knowledge of the content and the process of teaching should reflect in what you write when you think of this particular teacher and the subject she taught. Be reflective. Demonstrate that you paid attention in this class.

What did you learn that you still remember, even after all these years?

Essay responses to this particular assignment were varied and fascinating. First, I wanted to know what they actually retained from different developmental and behavioral theories we had discussed (Piaget, Vygotsky, Erikson, Skinner, etc.) And second, I wanted to know if I modeled good teaching. The process and classroom management are parts of good teaching also. Those essays were precious to me, and I kept them for a long time. Then, one day, I took each essay, and typed it on my computer verbatim—mistakes and all—with the name of the student on top. These "Obituary Essays" are all in a binder, and I'm keeping them.

One gentleman, Bob Withrow, who I believe was managing a restaurant in Boise at the time; wrote the following comments:

"Only one thing is more brutal than night school, Saturday school. Or so I thought. There is a good chance that was a mistake, at least when it came to her class. She came the first day too perky, too familiar. It was almost annoying. I stayed. I even bought into the style."

I chuckled when I read it. But the most important part to me was what he wrote at the very end of his essay:

"Most of all, I remember the respect and dignity afforded to all the students. That is what I learned I guess."

Well, Mr. Withrow, wherever you are, you captured the essence. All students, all human beings, deserve respect and dignity.

ACKNOWLEDGMENTS

I'm grateful for my family, friends, colleagues, neighbors, and just about anybody I've known throughout my life. If you recognize any of my characters in these short stories, it is because they are real. They have been part of my life, and I love and appreciate them all.

"No man is an island," said John Donne, English poet. We don't go through life alone without the support of others. As human beings we are all connected to each other—and I see myself as a little piece of a big puzzle woven into the tapestry of life.

MEET THE AUTHOR

Manijeh Badiozamani is a literary non-fiction writer. She was born in Iran and has lived in the United States for over fifty years. She earned a PhD from the University of Idaho, taught at the college level, and published her first book, *Family Tales from Tehran,* in 2019. This is her second book, a memoir in short stories.

She lives in Florida with her husband.